Filled

Rediscovering
Holy Spirit Baptism

K. Sheldon Bailey

Unless otherwise indicated, Bible quotations are taken from
the New King James Version®. Copyright © 1982 by Thomas Nelson.
Used by permission. All rights reserved.

Scriptures from the Easy English Bible are from MissionAssist,
Copyright © MissionAssist 2016 –
Charitable Incorporated Organisation 1162807,
https://www.easyenglish.bible.

Scriptures marked (AMPC) are from the Amplified Bible,
Classic Edition. Copyright © 1954, 1958, 1962, 1964, 1965, 1987
by The Lockman Foundation.

Scriptures marked (NASB) are from the New American Standard Bible.
Copyright © 1960, 1962, 1963, 1968, 1971, 1972, 1973, 1975, 1977, 1995
by The Lockman Foundation.

Disciples' Pen Publishing
320 Pine Ave. Suite 803
Long Beach, CA 90802

K. Sheldon Bailey Ministries International
"Taking the Word, Teaching the World"
KSheldonBailey.org

Images:
Front and back cover water: OmniArt/Shutterstock.com
Front cover dove: Whitedovereleasecolorado.com
Back cover and interior dove: Lotus_Studio/Shutterstock.com

All Honor, Glory, Power,
Praise, and Appreciation to…

My Lord, my God
My Christ and King
My Keeper, my Comfort
My Everything!

Provider, Protector
My Joy and Peace
My Rock, my Ruler
Source of my need

My Master, my Strength
My Shelter, my Rest
My Savior and Shepherd
Elohim, Your Highness

My Helper, my Healer
My Life, my Lamb
Defender, Redeemer
Adonai, I AM

In Loving Memory of
Adrienne Florence Bailey
The "Moms"

Rarely does a day go by without
A thought of you visiting my mind.
It almost always brings a smile to my face.
But sometimes it brings a tear to my eye.

Thank you for your many sacrifices,
Thank you for your commitment to Christ,
Thank you for being loving, kind, and caring,
Thank you for your example of a Spirit-filled life.

I love you. I miss you.
And, I'll see you again!

SPECIAL ACKNOWLEDGMENTS

Valerie Browne, Dr. R. Wilks, Bishop E. Smith, Lola DuCree, Richard C. James, Dorothy James, Marvin L. Williams, Angie Marquez, Jeff Haynes, Pastor E. Clark, Ted Matt, Pastor R. Horne, Pastor T. Russell, Pastor D. Pocoroba, C. Woodard, Y. Peeples, and the many others who aid me in different ways in "Taking the Word, Teaching the World!" Ten thousand thanks to you all! I could not do what I do were it not for the role you all play in my life and ministry. I am truly grateful to God for you all!

AUNTIE V

I love you. I love talking with you and being inspired by your wisdom, your love, and your kindness. I love the time we spend together, be it short or long.

I love that you love people and that you are greatly loved by the people you love. I love that you love my silly attempts to be humorous. I love laughing with you.

I love the fact that you are in my life. My life is better because of your presence. Everyone's life is better because of your presence.

I could not be more grateful for all you do and say to encourage, inspire, and aid me in my quest to impact the lives of people everywhere for our risen Christ and King.

You are truly a special person to me with a special place in my life that will forever be unoccupied by another.

Love, hugs, kisses and hugs!

Nephew K.

TABLE OF CONTENTS

FOREWORD

Nearly twenty-five years ago, when I recognized there was an absence of consensus concerning the subject of Holy Spirit baptism, I felt a strong urge to learn as much about it as I could and to teach what I had learned to as many as I could.

I committed my life to Jesus in a church that believed in Holy Spirit baptism but did not teach on it extensively. A few years into my ten-year tenure there, I would come to recognize that my church and I didn't share an understanding of some of the manifestations, abilities, or attributes of the matter. At that time, this was not that big of a deal to me—namely because I had not yet come to know how tremendously important the matter of Holy Spirit baptism was to the individual Christian, the Christian church, and the body of Christ as a whole.

During my time there, and in subsequent years, I have heard people mocking many aspects of the filling of the Holy Spirit; some even going so far as to suggest that certain elements of it were "of the devil." Which of course is not true, simply because nothing that is of God can be "of the devil." Others offered legitimate questions for which I had no sound biblical answers for at the time.

However, I understood two things about their questions that apply to questions universally. The presence of questions only exists in the absence of answers. We only have questions because we don't have answers. When questions are satisfied with answers that may or may not be accurate, questions are quietly dissolved.

Secondly, I understood that when there are questions, there are voids and vacuums in the mind that can be occupied by that which is incorrect, incomplete, or the offering of someone's misunderstanding of the matter. Here are just a few of the questions that are common to the subject of Holy Spirit baptism:

- *Isn't every Christian filled with the Holy Spirit?*
- *Why do some people make a big deal of tongues?*
- *Doesn't the Bible say that not all have the gift of tongues?*
- *If tongues are so important, why didn't Jesus speak in tongues?*
- *Is it true that if I am not filled with the Holy Spirit or speak in tongues, I am not saved?*
- *Is tongues of the devil?*

When I knew that I would at some point be required to teach on the somewhat controversial subject of Holy Spirit baptism, I remember requesting of God to *"help me answer all of the questions"* I was aware of. And over these more than two decades, He has not only enabled me to answer those questions, but the Lord also has been gracious in giving me insight into other areas of this most important matter.

In addition to spelling out with crystal clarity the answers to common questions like those above and addressing some of the myths and misconceptions of Holy Spirit baptism, I believe the Lord has unlocked hidden treasures and revealed many mysteries of Holy Spirit baptism in the pages that follow.

INTRODUCTION

J esus says in **John 10:10,** *"The thief does not come except to steal, and to kill, and to destroy."*

According to Jesus and the order of what He offers in this verse, the primary aim of our arch enemy is to steal. Be it from the world, from the church, or from the individual Christian, the devil's principal purpose is to leave us without something of value we have been given.

Typically, when we think about someone stealing we think about them stealing something tangible like a car, a wallet, a bicycle, or money from our bank account. While the devil may influence people to steal those types of things from us, the devil himself is not primarily interested in stealing our tangible valuables. No, he's interested in something far more valuable than all of the riches in the world combined.

More than anything else, the devil's desire is to steal the truth of the Word of God from the heart and mind of men and from the church of the true and living God. The devil doesn't steal spiritual truth from us so that *he* can benefit directly; he steals truth so that he can benefit indirectly by what we no longer are in possession of. Stealing spiritual truth from us doesn't help the devil because the father of lies has no use for truth. He steals truth from us so that we won't have it to use against him or to benefit in the way the Father intends.

When Satan disguised as a snake makes his debut in the Bible, what we find him doing in the Garden of Eden is shoplifting the Word of God from the heart of Eve.

Genesis 3:1-6
Now the serpent was more cunning than any
beast of the field which the Lord God had made.
² And he said to the woman, "Has God indeed said,
'You shall not eat of every tree of the garden'?"
And the woman said to the serpent,
"We may eat the fruit of the trees of the garden;
³ but of the fruit of the tree which is in the midst of the
garden, God has said, 'You shall not eat it,
nor shall you touch it, lest you die.' "
⁴ Then the serpent said to the woman, "You will <u>not</u> surely
die. ⁵ For God knows that in the day you eat of it your eyes
will be opened, and you will be like God, knowing good and
evil." ⁶ So when the woman saw that the tree was good for
food, that is was pleasant to the eyes, and a tree desirable to
make one wise, she took of its fruit
and ate. She also gave to her husband
with her, and he ate.

We understand that the disobedience of Adam and Eve is what allowed sin to enter, not only them but also into the earth that they had been given to rule and have dominion over. But the question is, *how* did the devil cause them to disobey the instructions God had made very clear to Adam?

One might say the devil did so through deception and trickery. While there was indeed deception and a trait of trickery used, it was actually through thievery that Satan stole the truth of God's Word when he said to Eve, **"You shall <u>*not*</u> surely die."** When he *removed* the original meaning of what God said, he stole the truth from their life. While deception and trickery were accessories to the crime, thievery was the crime itself.

What we see the devil doing when he is introduced in the Scriptures and introduces himself to Eve is stealing from her and Adam the truth God had given to protect and bless them. When Satan is *first* revealed the *first* thing we find him doing is, stealing the Word of God from the children of God!

This is one reason why Jesus in **John 10:10** identifies the devil as a "thief" who "comes to steal" even before He talks about him killing and destroying. When he *came* to Eve, he came for no other reason than to steal from her and Adam the life-giving Word of Truth.

He didn't *come* to steal fruit or flowers from her garden. He wasn't aiming for any of the fowls, fish, insects, or animals who were all under their care. His plan was not to pilfer their pet hippos. Neither was the king of demons interested in *any* of the tangible possessions of their hand. No, his agenda was to steal the more valuable, intangible treasure from their heart, which was the Word of God. Far more than wanting to steal *things* from our *hand*, the devil wants to steal *truth* from our *heart*.

He cannot benefit from the tools of truth that God uses to build us up, or the Word that serves as a sword and weapon of our warfare, so he seeks to steal them so that we cannot have them to be built up and battle ready.

According to Jesus, thousands of years later, "the thief" had not, nor has not changed his method of operation. The devil *still* comes to steal from us as children of God. Whether it's stealing from us as individuals, or us as the church, a body of believers.

In the life of the Christian who is saved and on their way to heaven when we leave earth, when it comes to tools, weapons, rights, and benefits, the single most important thing to us that the devil is interested in stealing from us is the truth about Holy Spirit baptism.

I have long believed that the devil has a *"take what I can get"* mentality. If he cannot keep us from eternal life in heaven, he will settle for stealing our abundant life on earth or our high level of effectiveness for God while we are on earth. And if the devil cannot keep us from receiving *all* of what God has for us, he will settle for keeping us from possessing *some* of what God has and desires for us.

And concerning the all-too-important topic of Holy Spirit baptism, the devil has stolen much of the truth of the matter. He has done so in a number of ways, including keeping the subject of Holy Spirit baptism completely away from many Christians, limiting the teaching, understanding, and conversations about it, and by causing chaos, confusion, and division in our discussions of it.

It is imperative for us to understand that everything that is of the devil is designed and purposed to steal, kill, and destroy. Chaos seeks to steal, kill, and destroy harmony and order; confusion seeks to steal, kill, and destroy clarity and understanding; and of course, division seeks to steal, kill, and destroy agreement and unity.

And while everything the devil seeks to steal is of value to us (though not to him), **"the unity of the faith"** (what we believe) is of utmost importance to him because the place of unity is where the Lord bestows His blessings and imparts His power—blessings and power Satan also wants to steal and deprive us of possessing.

However, *Filled* is purposed, biblically empowered, and insightfully equipped to take back the truths concerning Holy Spirit baptism. *Filled* will help the body of Christ throughout the world to recover that which has been stolen by revealing that which has been hidden. This book will lead many back to the blessings and benefits that accompany being *Filled* with the Holy Spirit!

My prayer to the Father has been that those who read this book will have all of their questions answered, their confusion quieted, and all of their doubts cast out. I have also asked that those who read *Filled* would do so with thirst for truth and a come-what-may commitment to embracing truth when it visits and reveals itself. And I pray that you, through the pages of this book, would come to experience the baptism of the Holy Spirit and be equipped to lead others into this extremely important and intimate experience.

God's best!

DEDICATION

Filled is dedicated to every
Christian, in America and abroad,
who has a desire to impact the
life of people with the power of God.

CHAPTER 1

BAPTISM, BAPTISM, BAPTISM?

**Therefore, leaving the discussion of the elementary princi-
ples of Christ, let us go on to perfection, not laying again
the foundation of repentance from dead works and of faith
toward God, of the doctrine of baptisms, of laying on of
hands, of resurrection of the dead,
and of eternal judgment.
Hebrews 6:1-2**

My personal introduction to the subject of baptism came in a traditional, somewhat conservative Christian church in the late 80s. After a brief explanation of water baptism that I would experience in the weeks to follow, I later learned more about water baptism in the six-week new members' class. Beyond that, I do not recall receiving any in-depth teaching on the other types of baptisms, their purpose, their function, what they mean, who performs them, when they are performed, or why they are important. Consequently, I spent the formative years of my Christianity without having a sound, biblically educated understanding of the different types of baptisms that are evident in the Scriptures.

Over the years, I have come to recognize that, like me, many Christians, at varying levels of maturity, had neither been taught the types and differences of these baptisms and therefore do not have a firm understanding of the subject. According to the apostle Paul, the different baptisms are basic to our faith and should, therefore, be taught early on.

There is a tendency for the words *basic* and *elementary* to offend seasoned Christians when presented. But they should not because there are times in our life, be it in our career, our marriage, or our relationship with God, when we simply need to *get back to basics*. Doing so does not undo anything we have accomplished or lessen our level of maturity; it simply prepares us to go even higher in the area in which we are revisiting the basics.

LAYING THE FOUNDATION

Because Holy Spirit baptism is elementary to Christianity, it means it is also foundational to the Christian faith. Foundations are extremely important. In fact, foundations are the most important part of every structure. The architects and builders of the world's tallest building would all agree that the foundation of that building, though not the most *impressive part,* is without question the most *important part.* Such is the case with elementary things.

There is a tendency to think elementary things are not very important and can be done without. But the contrary is true. Elementary things cannot be done without because they are the foundation upon which other things are established. No one receives a college degree without first having learned the teachings of elementary school.

The author of the book of Hebrews communicates the importance of teachings that are elementary and foundational to our faith. However, he then says that we are to leave *the discussion of the elementary* things and *lay not again the foundation.* This isn't to say we should leave those things that are elementary and foundational without first laying them. That would not allow for building, or, it would not allow for that which is built to be strong and lasting. Instead, the writer is saying that we should lay those teachings that are foundational and *then* leave them; not having to revisit and readdress the same basic elements of our faith, as a body. When a builder lays a foundation, he never goes back to lay it again. However, if he has not laid it properly, he will not be permitted by the building inspector to move on to the next phase of the building project.

We as the body of Christ as a whole are still striving to properly lay the foundational teaching of Holy Spirit baptism. Consequently, we are delayed in being built up to be the tall, strong skyscrapers God desires. **Colossians 2:7** talks about us being **"rooted and built up in Him, and established in Him."** Being "rooted" has to do with the foundation. The foundation of a tree is its roots. And the taller the tree, the deeper the roots. It's the same for buildings. The taller the building, the deeper the foundation must descend into the earth. And it's no different for us as believers and followers of Jesus the Christ. If we are going to be **"built up,"** we must first be **"rooted"** in the foundational facts of our faith.

Notice the order of these two elements in the verse, **"rooted"** first, and then, **"built up."** The benefits of being **"built up"** on and **"rooted"** in solid teaching of Holy Spirit baptism will greatly aid us as individual Christians, individual Christian churches, and the entire Christian faith, in many ways. Among the ways we are aided include spiritual growth that helps to keep us from falling away from the faith, and spiritual power that equips us to perform the miracles Jesus performed. It will also go a long way towards helping the body of Christ as a whole be the salt and light that is purposed to influence and win the world to Christ!

The Spirit of God inspired the writer of Hebrews to address the need for a firm understanding of the elementary things of the faith (including Holy Spirit baptism) because God knew this instruction would be necessary for the body of Christ in the nowadays of history. As a whole, we are striving for unity on even the foundational teachings of our faith. If and when we achieve this unity we will be able to move on to the greater, deeper, more impactful, world-changing elements of our faith.

This is extremely important because the harvest of the world is truly plentiful in souls and ripe for picking. As we come into agreement on which tools are essential for getting the job done, as laborers we will multiply as Christians from millions to billions!

It is impossible to grow,
If we are still being taught,
What we should already know.

The subject of Holy Spirit baptism truly is a basic, elementary matter of Christianity that should be taught early on to new Christians. Nothing reveals this like the passage in Hebrews that lists baptisms (plural—indicating there is more than one type) under the category of **"elementary principles."** Also, the statement, **"let us go on to maturity,"** says to us that every type of *baptism* should be understood and taught while we are yet young in our Christian faith.

However, many Christians who have been on the path of Christian living for quite some time are still without a firm understanding of the different types of baptisms, who performs them, their purpose, and how they function. This is the reason why there is a great deal of discussion, disagreement, and debate about the subject, even among scholars.

One of the things the devil seeks to do (and unfortunately, has done) is cause the church to be mired in the misunderstanding of the different types of baptisms, thereby preventing us from *going on* to more mature matters or **"the deep things of God"** within our Christian faith. This chapter is designed to bring clarity in understanding the different types of baptisms. Moving on to **"the deep things of God"** the apostle Paul writes about is important but impossible because there can be no moving on to maturity until certain foundational truths are laid; truths that are the platform upon which all building must take place.

There is a great move of God on the horizon that will open our hearts and our minds, and propel the Christian church to another level of power and greatness, for the glory of God! And this great move begins with us rediscovering some truths about Holy Spirit baptism and how it differs from the other types of baptism.

EXAMINING THE DIFFERENT TYPES OF BAPTISMS

Let's take a look at three of the four types of baptisms the Bible references that apply to Christians and New Testament times.

(The one type of baptism we will not go into detail about is one that has been referred to as "the baptism of suffering." Scriptural references to this particular baptism that speaks of a time of trials, tribulations, or persecution can be found in **Luke 12:50, Matthew 20, 22, 23,** *and other places. I also write extensively about trials and tribulations in my book,* Trouble.*)*

There has long been confusion, controversy, and questions concerning just how many different types of baptisms there are in the Scriptures of Christianity. Many hold to the basic knowledge of just one type of baptism, and that being water baptism. Others embrace water baptism while believing also in the invisible baptism into the body of Christian believers, which is a work of the Holy Spirit. And there are yet others who believed in both water baptism and baptism of the Holy Spirit into the body of Christ, while believing also in a third baptism, which is Holy Spirit baptism.

Many have been taught that the Holy Spirit's baptizing work into the body of believers and Holy Spirit baptism are one and the same. It is very easy to understand how Christians can believe this, however, there is a difference between being baptized *by* the Holy Spirit, and being baptized *in or with* the Holy Spirit. Also, these two separate baptisms have a different purpose. But again, each of these baptisms are elementary in nature.

I will explain the three in more detail later in this chapter, but here is a brief description of the three different types of baptism and where they are represented in the Bible:

1) Baptism of the Holy Spirit. (Performed <u>by the Holy Spirit</u>.) **1 Corinthians 12:13, Galatians 3:27, Colossians 2:12.**

2) Water baptism. (Performed <u>by man</u>.) **Matthew 3:11, 16, 28:19; Mark 1:8-9, Luke 3:21, John 1:31, 33; Acts 2:38, 41, 8:12, 13, 36-38, 9:18, 10:47-48, 16:15, 33, 18:8, 19:3-5, 1 Corinthians 1:14, 16.**

3) Holy Spirit baptism. (Performed <u>by Jesus</u>.) **Matthew 3:11, 20:22, 23; Mark 1:8, 10:38, 39; Luke 3:16; 11:13, John 1:33, 7:37-39; Acts 1:5, 2:4, 38, 9:17, 10:44-47, 11:16, 8:16-18, 19:6.**

Each of these three types of baptisms are exclusive of the other. And for the Christian, only one is guaranteed to occur and that is the first one referenced, which is the baptism *by* the Holy Spirit. This inaugural work of the Holy Spirit invisibly places us into the body of Christ and makes us a part of the Christian family.

The baptism *by* the Holy Spirit occurs first because it is the very first thing that happens when a person repents (vows to turn from a life of sin) and believes in Jesus as *the* Savior of the whole world. In the moment this takes place, instantly, invisibly, and without any earthly fanfare, a person is made a child of God with all of the rights, benefits, and privileges of Christianity, including the promise of eternal life in heaven! And although we do not see anything, feel anything, or sense anything on earth, there is a celebration that takes place in heaven!

This is why Jesus says in **Luke 15:7, "I say to you that likewise there will be more joy in heaven over one sinner who repents than over ninety-nine just persons who need no repentance."** That **"joy in heaven"** is the angels of God celebrating because of the new addition that has been *placed into* the family of God *by* the baptizing work of the Holy Spirit. **Verse 10** goes on to reveal what happens in heaven when a person is added to the Christian family, or the body of Christ, on earth: **"...there is joy in the presence of the angels of God over one sinner who repents."**

THE ORDER OF THE THREE BAPTISMS

Although the baptism *by* the Holy Spirit always occurs first, there is no set order for which of the other types of baptism must follow. In fact, neither of the other two baptisms may ever take place in the life of a Christian. However, when possible (unless a person is coming to Christ in the waning days or moments of their life, or are physically incapable of being immersed in water for some reason) a person most certainly should seek to be baptized *by man* in water in obedience to the Holy Scriptures. As well, a person should seek to be baptized *by Jesus* in the Holy Spirit in order to enjoy and be equipped with all that accompanies baptism *in* the Holy Spirit.

After a new Christian has been immediately baptized (or placed into the body of Christian believers) by the Holy Spirit, there is no set order in which the other two baptisms should or will take place. In the Scriptures we find Christians being baptized by man in water, and sometime later being baptized by Jesus with the Holy Spirit **(Acts 8:12-17)**. And we also find instances when people were baptized by Jesus with the Holy Spirit *before* being baptized in water **(Acts 10:44-48)**. So, there is no particular order in which being baptized *in* water, or being baptized *in* the Holy Spirit must occur.

What we will find in **Acts 10** proves the point that Holy Spirit baptism is an elementary issue, and supports my assertion that it can take place even in the life of brand-new Christians.

The story of **Acts 10** details the time in history when the Lord led the apostle Peter to the home of a gentleman named Cornelius. Cornelius was a good man who loved God and compassionately and generously gave to people who were in need. For quite some time he had been in prayer to God. One day the Lord responded, and His response would lead to a visit from Peter and a few other disciples that would forever change the life of Cornelius, his family, friends, and others they would later come in contact with. While Peter was sharing the good news about Jesus, this happened:

> **⁴⁴ While Peter was still speaking these words, the Holy Spirit fell upon all those who heard the word. ⁴⁵ And those of the circumcision who believed were astonished, as many as came with Peter, because the gift of the Holy Spirit had been poured out on the Gentiles also. ⁴⁶ For they heard them speak with tongues and magnify God. Then Peter answered, ⁴⁷ "Can anyone forbid water, that these should not be baptized who have received the Holy Spirit just as we have?"**

This is a fascinating passage! And it is perfect for making the points of there being three different baptisms and how they are elementary to the Christian faith and intended even for those who are new to Christ.

We find this latter truth in the fact that Cornelius and his family and friends were hearing the Gospel of Jesus for the very first time. Undoubtedly, they believed what they heard, and consequently they were saved. But before they could be taught anything else about Christianity, they experienced the baptism of the Holy Spirit! Despite the fact that they were literally *newborn babes in Christ Jesus*, the Holy Spirit fell upon them, proving the experience of Holy Spirit baptism (or, being *filled with the Holy Spirit*) is truly basic and elementary in nature.

But also we find in this situation three of the four baptisms we're making a case for in this chapter. The first, baptism *by* the Holy Spirit, which is the invisible baptism that takes place as soon as people place their faith in Jesus for salvation. Another baptism, that of being baptized *with* or *in* the Holy Spirit, seen in **verse 44**. And yet another baptism, that of water, which is mentioned in **verse 47**. In fact, water baptism *and* Holy Spirit baptism are both mentioned in **verse 47**.

The confusion comes in not realizing there is a difference between being baptized <u>by the Holy Spirit</u> into the body of Christ, and being baptized <u>by Jesus</u> *with* the Holy Spirit. With a close look and careful consideration, we can clearly see these two baptisms are separate and distinct from one another.

In order to see and understand the difference we must first understand their purpose.

SPIRIT BAPTISM

1. Baptism of the Holy Spirit (the work of the Holy Spirit) is purposed to place new Christians *in* Christ and therefore into the family of God as heirs of salvation.

1 Corinthians 12:13
For <u>by</u> one Spirit we were all baptized
<u>into one body</u>—whether Jews or Greeks,
whether slaves or free—and have all been
made to drink of one Spirit.

The word **"by"** tells us *Who* is doing the baptizing, and **"into one body"** tells us *what* or *where* we are baptized into. The Spirit of God is doing the baptizing, and He is baptizing (or placing us) into the body of Christ. This is not water baptism, or baptism *in* the Holy Spirit. This is the saving baptism that is performed **"by"** the Holy Spirit.

Another verse that speaks of this particular baptism is **Ephesians 4:5**, which says, **"One Lord, one faith, one baptism."**

Some have used this verse to indicate that there is literally only one baptism. However, it is quite easy to demonstrate that there is more than *one baptism.* Paul using the word *baptism* in plural form in **Hebrews 6:2** would be enough evidence, but also, there are places in the Bible (**Acts 10** being one of them) that reveal Holy Spirit baptism by Jesus and water baptism by man taking place exclusive of the other. **Ephesians 4:5** is not talking about there literally being only one baptism just as it is not intended to convey that there is literally only one type of lord, or one type of faith.

We know there are many different types of lords because Jesus is **"Lord of *lords.*"** We know also there are many different types of faiths because there are many different types of religions and gods that people believe or place faith in. So, when the apostle Paul wrote about there being **"one Lord, one faith, (and) one baptism,"** he was saying that there is only one *saving* Lord, one *saving* faith, and one *saving* baptism. The *saving* baptism is not water baptism performed by man, or the baptism of Holy Spirit performed by Jesus; it's the baptism performed *by* the Holy Spirit, placing us into the body of Christ.

WATER BAPTISM

2. Water baptism (the work of man) is purposed to be an outward demonstration of the inward decision one has made to repent from their sins, believe in Jesus **(Mark 1:15)**, and live a new life in Him and for Him. It symbolizes the death of the old sinful man and his old sinful ways, his burial, and the resurrection of a new person who genuinely intends to live a new life in Christ. The Bible paints a beautiful picture of what water baptism represents.

> **Therefore we were buried with**
> **Him through baptism into death, that just as**
> **Christ was raised from the dead by the glory**
> **of the Father, even so we also should**
> **walk in newness of life.**
> **Romans 6:4**

The old man and his old sinful ways are symbolically buried when one is immersed in water during baptism; and the raising up out of the water is a reflection of the new birth wherein the new resurrected person determines to live a new life in Christ.

Another verse that gives us a glimpse into what water baptism symbolizes is **2 Corinthians 5:17** which states, **"...if anyone is in Christ, he is a new creation; old things are passed away; behold, all things have become new."**

This verse also reveals the work of two of the three baptisms without using the word *baptism*. The first type of baptism seen (which we previously addressed), the saving baptism which is performed by the Holy Spirit, and seen in the term **"in Christ."** At the point of salvation, the Holy Spirit *baptizes* or places us **"in Christ."** In doing so we are made a part of the family of God and become children of God.

The other type of baptism seen in the verse is *water baptism*. This symbolic baptism is represented in the phrase **"passed away."** In America, this term is commonly used when a person has died. The use of **"passed away"** in this verse is to signify the *death* of the old natural man and the resurrected rebirth of a new spiritual man in his place. It is this *born-again* person who is determined to live a new life in pursuit of the Christ-likeness of holiness.

BAPTISM BY THE CHRIST

3. Holy Spirit baptism performed by Jesus is a completely separate and distinct work from both; being baptized into the body of Christ by the Holy Spirit, and being baptized into water by another human.

Interestingly enough, the first New Testament mention of Jesus baptizing His followers in the Holy Spirit takes place in the same verse water baptism is mentioned.

I indeed baptize you with water unto repentance, but He who is coming after me is mightier than I, whose sandals I am not worthy to carry. He will baptize you with the Holy Spirit and fire.
Matthew 3:11

(This is another verse that draws a distinction between baptisms, proving in the process that there is more than "one baptism.")

The reference to **"fire"** is not an indication of another type of baptism, but simply an expression of what would be experienced when this prophecy was fulfilled on the day of Pentecost.

> **"Then there appeared to them divided tongues,
> as of <u>fire</u>, and one sat upon each of them.
> And they were all filled with the Holy Spirit…"**
> **Acts 2:3-4a**

This is the only time in the Scriptures when people were being filled/baptized with the Holy Spirit that *fire* is mentioned. This is what causes me to believe that John's reference to Jesus baptizing people with the Spirit and fire is one and the same thing.

But the purpose of Jesus baptizing His followers with the Holy Spirit is to empower us for service to Him and to equip us to live for Him.

> **But you shall receive *power* when the
> Holy Spirit has come upon (filled or baptized)
> you; and you shall be witnesses to Me in
> Jerusalem, and in all Judea and Samaria,
> and to the end of the earth.**
> **Acts 1:8**

When we give our life to God by repenting from our sin and placing our trust in Jesus as the Savior, we are instantly baptized *by* the Holy Spirit and placed into the eternal family of the Father.

When we in obedience get baptized in water *by* another person, we are showing whoever witnesses that baptism that we have made a decision to bury the old man and his old ways, and to **"walk in newness of life"** with Jesus as our Lord.

And when we are baptized in the Holy Spirit *by* Jesus, we are empowered and equipped to grow at the pace that God wants us to grow, live the life that God wants us to live, and make the impact on others that God wants us to make!

THE CHALLENGE OF MIND CHANGING

It has been my prayer that the body of Christ would come to understand the different types of baptisms that I have spelled out in this opening chapter. I have long believed, and seen it proven, that when people love the Word of God and are presented with truth in clarity, they embrace it. Even if it means going against the grain of what they've always been taught.

I personally know how challenging that can be. I spent the first ten years of my Christian life attending a denominational church that didn't believe there was a difference between the baptizing work of the Holy Spirit and the baptizing work of Jesus. But when the Lord made this matter plain to me in His Word, I had to place my trust in Him and hold tightly to what He revealed to me. Trusting and following truth often calls for us to swim against the current of former teachings. But doing so always leads us to an area of the ocean we have yet to explore! A deep area that is full of wonderful findings!

If this chapter has enabled you to recognize the difference between the baptism performed *by* the Holy Spirit and the baptism performed *by* Jesus, the following chapters will further act to bring clarity to areas of cloudiness. So, without further ado…here's chapter 2!

CHAPTER 2

FILLED

**When the Day of Pentecost had fully come,
they were all with one accord in one place.
And suddenly there came a sound from heaven
as of a rushing mighty wind, and it filled the whole
house where they were sitting. Then there appeared to them
divided tongues, as of fire, and one sat upon each
of them. And they were all filled with the Holy Spirit
and began to speak with other tongues,
as the Spirit gave them utterance.**
Acts 2:1-4

Sometime after the first century, when the New Testament church was established in the book of Acts, there arose a controversy concerning the Holy Spirit. This controversy included a number of factors. Among them was the issue of whether or not every Christian is **"filled with the Holy Spirit"** upon repentance from sin and faith in Jesus as the Savior of the world.

Some, in support of the belief that every Christian was indeed filled at the point of salvation, point to **John 7:39** wherein the apostle John sought to explain the comment made by Jesus which states, **"He who believes in Me, as the Scripture has said, out of his heart will flow rivers of living water" (John 7:38)**. John's response in the following verse says, **"But this He (Jesus) spoke concerning the Spirit, whom those believing in Him would receive; for the Holy Spirit was not yet given, because Jesus was not yet glorified."**

For many people, then and now, John's clarification of what Jesus meant serves as solid support for the fact that every Christian is **"filled with the Holy Spirit"** simply because they are Christians. However, others, pointing to a number of different passages we will visit later, hold to the belief that every Christian *can* be filled, but, not every Christian *is* or *has been* filled.

This latter group, like me, believes what John revealed is that everyone who trusts in Jesus as their Savior is given a measure of the Holy Spirit wherein He takes up residence in the Christian in the instance of salvation and immediately begins to fulfill His purpose in their life.

> **But you are not in the flesh but in the Spirit,**
> **if indeed the Spirit of God dwells in you.**
> **Now if anyone does not have the Spirit**
> **of Christ, he is not His.**
> **Roman 8:9**

This is another verse that has accidentally caused confusion and controversy concerning the *filling* of the Holy Spirit; leading many to believe that if they have received Jesus as their Savior and therefore belong to Him, they are also *filled* with the Holy Spirit. But what is important to understand is that there is a difference between the Holy Spirit *dwelling* in us and the Holy Spirit *filling* us.

It's true, if a person does not have the Spirit of God *dwelling* in him, he does not belong to God and is therefore not saved. But this verse does not say, *"If anyone is not filled he is not God's, or he is not saved."* Let me be clear, it is 100 percent possible to be saved and not be filled with the Holy Spirit. This is because the Holy Spirit *dwelling* in us is one thing, but Him *filling* us is something completely different.

In fact, in the original Greek offering of the words *fill* and *dwell* (and any variation of them) they have different meanings.

"And they were all *filled* with the Holy Spirit
and began to speak in other tongues…"
Acts 2:4

The Greek word for the word *filled* found in the very first occurrence of Holy Spirit baptism is a word we would pronounce, *play'-tho*, and it simply means *full*.

However, the Greek word for *dwell* found in **Romans 8:9** is a word we would pronounce, *oy-keh'-o*, and it means, *to reside in*, or to *occupy (as in a house)*. **First Corinthians 3:16** provides us with a vivid picture of the Holy Spirit *occupying* the Christian in this particular context in posing the question, **"Do you not know that you are the temple of God and that the Spirit of God <u>dwells</u> in you?"**

2 Timothy 1:14
That good thing which was committed
to you, keep by the Holy Spirit
who <u>dwells</u> in you.

Here, in Paul's penning to Timothy, we find this same idea using a Greek word we would pronounce, *en-oy-keh'-o*. The resemblance to the Greek word found in **Romans 8:9** and **1 Corinthians 3:16** indicates these words are related. *Oy-keh'-o*, means *to reside in*, or to *occupy*; *en-oy-keh'-o* means to *inhabit*. Of course, *to reside in, occupy,* or *inhabit* are all synonymous terms, but neither of them necessarily means the place of residence, occupation, or habitation is *full*. Just as it is possible for a home to have furniture *occupying* one or two rooms and the home not be *filled* with furniture, it is also possible for the Holy Spirit to reside in us as His temple, but we not be *filled* with the Holy Spirit. But again, this does not mean we are not saved or don't belong to God. The fact that the

Holy Spirit *dwells* in us even without *filling* us means we do indeed belong to God and are heirs of salvation.

The *indwelling* of God's Spirit instantly takes place in the moment we place our trust in Jesus to save us from the penalty of our sin, which is eternal death. However, this indwelling *residency*, as important as it is, isn't the *fullness* of the Holy Spirit, or, it isn't all of the Holy Spirit that there is to be had by the Christian.

In a chapter to come, I will point out examples from the Bible of Christians who had been saved varying lengths of time (from days to decades) and had received the *indwelling* of the Holy Spirit, but had not yet been filled or received the *fullness* of the Holy Spirit. But first, in support of this possibility, let's carefully consider the word, *filled.*

Filled is a common word. However, it is also a very curious word in the context it is presented in **Acts 2:4, "And they were all *filled* with the Holy Spirit..."** The commonality of the word "filled" can subtract from the curiousness of its use in this text. Common words are often deprived of the careful consideration they deserve—a consideration given to uncommon or complex words. Because common words are often slighted, we sometimes miss the message they seek to share with us.

Filled is a regular, everyday word and the practice of *filling* things is a regular, everyday practice. Every day, people everywhere are *filling* up tanks with gas, cups with coffee, glasses with water, baby bottles with milk, and pitchers with beverages of all sorts. Our common practice of *filling* things up and using the words *fill, filling, or filled* doesn't allow us to consider or question what it means to be "*filled* **with the Holy Spirit**," nor the alternative to being *filled.*

The word *filled* is used in place of expressing a particular measurement such as one-half or three-fourths. Such measurements allow for more of whatever is being measured. But the word *filled* is not a numerical offering and it therefore does not represent or indicate a fraction. When something is *filled*, it means something is occupied fully and completely and not just fractionally or in part. Fractions mean there is yet room for adding or increase. However, when something is *filled* it means it is whole and there is no room or space for occupation because maximum capacity has been reached.

The word *filled* is typically only used when there is an alternative for a fraction or a lesser amount. When one desires not to settle for a lesser amount we *fill it up*, or ask for a *refill*.

The use of the word *"filled"* as it pertains to the Holy Spirit signifies that having a fraction, or a lesser amount, is also a possibility. If there was no such possibility of a fraction or a lesser amount of the Holy Spirit the word *"filled"* would not have been used in **Acts 2:4** (or similar verses). Instead, the Spirit would have inspired Luke to write, *"And they all had the Holy Spirit,"* in lieu of, **"And they were all *filled* with the Holy Spirit."**

The former would have conveyed there is no measure and simply *having* the Holy Spirit is all there is to it and nothing more or different is possible. But because the word *"filled"* was used, doing so communicates the existence of a lesser amount of the Holy Spirit.

The possibility of a lesser than *filled* amount of the Holy Spirit is also communicated corporately by the disciples when they sought assistance in aiding the widows who were being neglected. Look at the qualities expressed in **Acts 6:1-4** that the disciples desired of the candidates who would be chosen for this most important area of ministry:

Now in those days, when the number of disciples was multiplying, there arose a complaint against the Hebrews by the Hellenists, because their widows were neglected in the daily distribution. [2] Then the twelve summoned the multitude of the disciples and said, "It is not desirable that we should leave the Word of God and serve tables. [3] Therefore, brethren, seek out from among you seven men of good reputation, <u>full</u> of the

**Holy Spirit and wisdom, whom we may
appoint over this business; ⁴ but we will give
ourselves continually to prayer and to the
ministry of the word.”**

The disciples were deliberate in communicating their desire for those who would be considered for the ministry responsibility of helping the widows be **“…full of the Holy Spirit.”** If this wasn't exactly what the disciples had in mind, it would have been easy to simply say, *“Find us seven fellows who have a good reputation and the Holy Spirit…” Instead,* they were intentional in their expression that one of the necessities for the job was the seven guys be *filled with the Holy Spirit*, and not just have a measure of the Holy Spirit.

FILLED IS NOT A MEASUREMENT

In speaking of Jesus and His relationship with the Holy Spirit, **John 3:34** provides further support for the fact that it is possible to possess only a portion of the Holy Spirit, or, a measure of Him.

> **For He whom God has sent
> speaks the words of God:
> for God gives <u>not</u> the Spirit
> <u>by measure</u> to Him.**

In this verse (one of the few in which we see the fullness of the Godhead represented in one verse) it says the Father did not give the Son the Spirit **“by measure.”** Although it says Jesus was given the Holy Spirit without measure (or, in fullness), the very fact that *measure* is mentioned means it is possible for Christians to only have a measure of the Holy Spirit, and not be *filled*. This doesn't mean a Christian can never be filled or enjoy the fullness of the

Holy Spirit. It simply indicates being filled is not the only possibility when it comes to us possessing the Holy Spirit.

It's important to understand this because we don't pursue what we already think we are in possession of. If we are under the impression that we were **"filled with the Holy Spirit"** when we gave our life to Christ, we won't seek to be filled because we already believe we have been filled. No one looks for a gas station with a full tank of gas. In the same way, if we think our Holy Ghost gas tank is already filled, we won't look to the Lord to have Him, *fill* us up!

Check out the Easy English translation of **John 3:34:**

> **He that God has sent speaks God's words.**
> **God <u>fills Him completely</u> with God's Spirit.**

I love that translation because it adds clarity and simplicity. I love the following new, previously unheard of translation, as well:

> **"He that God has sent speaks the Word of God.**
> **And, His Father fills Him completely,**
> **without fraction, without measure,**
> **without room for more;**
> **to the utmost maximum capacity,**
> **without space for additional occupancy."**
> **John 3:34—KSBMIPT**
> *(K. Sheldon Bailey Make It Plain Translation)*

(What's the problem? Everyone else has a translation, why can't I? There is the, KJV, NIV, AMP, EET, CAT, DOG, LMNOP, and the QRSTUV translations. Why can't there be a, KSBMIP translation?)

Of course, as was the case with Jesus, it is possible for Christians to also have the Spirit without measure, which is what being *filled* is all about. Upon trusting in and committing our life to God by repentance from sin and faith in Jesus as the Christ, nine times out of ten people receive the Spirit only by measure in that moment.

(However, there is another baptizing work that is performed at that time, and we will see that in a later chapter.)

It is absolutely 100 percent true that when a person decides to trust in Jesus as their Savior, the Holy Spirit comes and takes up residence in them. This is a very important occurrence in the life of the Christian, because it signifies that we have been redeemed from the penalty of our sin (eternal death), and we now identify as being children of God. Again, the following verse makes this clear.

> **But you are not in the flesh but in the Spirit,**
> **if indeed the Spirit of God dwells *in* you.**
> **Now if anyone does not have the**
> **Spirit of Christ, he is none of His.**
> **Romans 8:9**

Every Christian has the Holy Spirit of God dwelling in them. There is no question about that. But this *dwelling* is not the *filling* or the *baptism* of the Holy Spirit. This is the basic measure of the Spirit given by God in the moment one entrusts their life to Christ Jesus for salvation.

There are rare instances when people get *filled* with the Holy Spirit at the time they give their life to Christ, but this is more of an exception than the rule. *(We will also see an example of this later.)* But being *filled* does not always take place in the moment of repentance and faith in Jesus.

MORE PLEASE!

The difference between having the Holy Spirit without measure *(being filled)* and having only a measure of the Spirit *(which is given to every born-again Christian)* is being able to do more, with more; and being able to enjoy and benefit to the fullest from all that the Holy Spirit offers with Himself.

For example, **Ephesians 3:16** talks about being **"strengthened with might through His Spirit in the inner man."** Having a measure of the Holy Spirit provides us with *some* **"might"** to live the Christian life, but being *filled* with the Holy Spirit will provide us with more **"might"** for the fights of the Christian life. More **"might"** means more **"strength"** and more **"strength in our inner man"** which is our spiritual man, means fewer defeats and more victories over our fleshly, natural man. This is extremely helpful in our quest to grow in Christ-likeness and live holy lives before a Holy God. And of course, holiness is important because, "**... without which no man shall see the Lord."**

The Greek word for **"might"** reveals a great deal as it pertains to how we're helped in fighting against our flesh and its sinful tendencies, the world and its sinful influences, and our ability to exercise the power of the Holy Spirit.

1. *Strength power, ability*
   a. *Inherent power, power residing inward that is exerted or exercised.*
   b. *Power for performing miracles.*
   c. *Moral power and excellence of soul.*

As we prepare to conclude this chapter, a broader look at **Ephesians 3** provides one final piece of evidence that being *filled* with the Holy Spirit is not an automatic occurrence upon salvation, but a subsequent work that God desires to perform in every Christian who is thirsty for all He has to offer in the form of Himself.

> **May (God) grant you out of the rich treasury of riches of His glory, to be strengthened with might through His Spirit in the inner man, [17] that Christ may dwell in your hearts through faith; that you, being rooted and grounded in love, [18] may be able to comprehend with all the saints what is the width and length and depth and height— [19] to know the love**

**of Christ which passes knowledge; that you
may be filled with all of the fullness of God.
Ephesians 3:16-19**

The term **"may be"** used in verses 18 and 19 is not a definite particle as the term "will be" is. And because **"may be"** is not a definite particle it does not speak of certainties or guarantees. It speaks of a hopeful desire that something will take place. Paul expressed his *hopeful desire* that the Christians in Ephesus would **"comprehend... the width, length, depth, and height"** of the **"love of Christ,"** but Paul knew that doing so wasn't a guarantee. In the same way, Paul went on to express the same *hopeful desire* in them being **"filled with all of the fullness of God."** Paul would not have possessed this *hopeful desire* of them being **"filled with all of the fullness of God"** if **"all of the fullness of God,"** particularly the fullness of His Holy Spirit, was a standard part of the salvation package.

**You shall be filled with all
of the fullness of God.**

Having a measure of the Holy Spirit certainly allows and enables us to exercise *some* strength and employ these powers with *some* degree of effectiveness. But being *filled* will allow us to not only be stronger, but to also have more strength and power to exercise. Again, if we have more, we can do more and be more. A car that is *filled* with fuel can travel further. A car that has a lesser amount of fuel can travel, but not as far. Having the fullness of something will enable us to enjoy more of what that something offers.

The Bible reveals a number of reasons the Father wants to give us the fullness of the Holy Spirit, and they all have to do with helping us in one way or another and enabling us to help others. Here are just a few of the ways and things the Holy Spirit helps us with.

John 14:26 - Teaches us and brings what we've learned to our remembrance.

Acts 1:8 – Empowers us

Acts 9:31 – Comforts us

Acts 10:38 – Anoints us for service

Romans 8:26 – Helps us with our weaknesses

Romans 14:17—Gives us peace

Romans 15:13 – Gives us hope

1 Corinthians 2:13 – Imparts spiritual wisdom

1 Thessalonians 1:6 – Gives us joy

With all of the ways and with all of the things the Holy Spirit helps us with, being *filled* with the Holy Spirit allows for these things and ways to operate in an even greater way for us, in us, and through us.

Trust in what the Scriptures reveal. And be open to receiving all of the Holy Spirit that is available to you as a servant of God and as a lover of Christ Jesus!

You'll be glad you did!

CHAPTER 3

BE FILLED

**"And do not be drunk with wine,
...but be filled with the Spirit,"
Ephesians 5:18**

The Lord would never tell a tree or a bee to *be* a tree or a bee because trees and bees are already trees and bees. In like manner, God never instructs us to "be" something we already are or will automatically become. If and when God instructs us to *be* something, it is because we are not that something by nature or without some additional action taking place.

In this verse, the very fact that the Holy Spirit inspired the apostle Paul to write and tell those in Ephesus who were already Christians to **"be filled with the Spirit"** indicates that it wasn't a given that they were already filled because they were saved.

It's no different with **1 Peter 1:16** that, in quoting God, admonishes Christians to **"be holy, for I am holy."** Verse 15 tells us what God has in mind with this particular admonition when it states:

**"But as the One Who called you is holy,
you yourselves also be holy in all your
conduct and manner of living."
1 Peter 1:15 (AMPC)**

In this case, the Lord is also instructing us to _be_ something that is not a standard element of the born-again experience. If every Christian were involuntarily made holy upon conversion to Christianity, there would be no need to pursue the maturity of holiness. Neither would there be any reason to pursue _being_ something God is planning on causing without our cooperation. We are instructed to **_"be holy"_** because holiness is the Christ-like character we must aim to make our own by way of consistent obedience to the Word of God. Holiness is not a reward or an award for having walked with God for a particular period of time.

This is also the case when it comes to being filled with the Holy Spirit. Because it is not a reward or a time-released occurrence (though it does occur at the time of salvation in rare instances as we will see shortly), God tells us to **"be filled,"** indicating that we, most often, must seek to be filled and be willing to be filled.

**Don't be drunk,
be filled!**

Discussions, disagreements, and debates on the topic of Holy Spirit baptism are not new to the twenty-first century church. These discussions, disagreements, and debates swirl around a few issues that theologians of denominational and nondenominational persuasions have disputed for centuries. While many men and women of God have not agreed wholeheartedly on the subject of Holy Spirit baptism, they have managed to maintain a mutual respect for each other while enjoying God-centered fellowship. Unfortunately, others have allowed the difference of belief to lead to divisions in the Christian body that have hindered the strength of our unity and, consequently, our effectiveness in winning a lost and spiritually dead world to Christ Jesus.

Unbiased Offering

The agenda of this book is not to pick and choose sides or to say who's wrong or who's right. The aim of *Filled* is simply to take a fresh look at the topic of Holy Spirit baptism in hopes that the Scriptures we value, trust in, and will revisit, will clear up any and all points of confusion or conflict. The aim of this particular chapter is to go deeper into scriptural consideration of whether or not there are different depths of relationships Christians can have with the Holy Spirit or if there is just one we all equally share at salvation.

We will see if the Bible supports the belief that all Christians are filled with the Holy Spirit at the time of conversion or if the filling can take place sometime later—be it days, months, or even decades. We will carefully consider both of these positions in this chapter and trust the very Spirit we are speaking of to provide clarity and understanding.

This is a very important matter because, if being filled with the Holy Spirit does *not* occur spontaneously at the time of trusting Jesus, or does not *always* occur at the point, but some have been under the impression that its does, they may go their entire life in Christ without possessing the power that accompanies being baptized in the Holy Spirit. This *power* is extremely significant to the life of the Christian because of all it enables us to do and how extremely helpful and necessary it is in order for us as Christians to (in the words of an old Army mantra) "be all we can be." Go Army!

(This reminds me of a T-shirt I saw a gentleman wearing at the VA clinic I visit. The shirt said, "Someone Told Me to 'Be All I Can Be' So…I Joined the Marines!" That was funny and it brought a grin to my face. But a moment later I felt sorry for the gentleman because he didn't take the person's advice; he became a Marine instead. It was hard but, yes, I forgave him. He had to take that T-shirt off though.)

The truth is, no one, military or civilian, can "be all they can be" without Jesus and without having the fullness of His Spirit dwelling on the inside of us.

Having the fullness of the power of God that comes with being filled with the Holy Spirit is extremely important for pastors and those of us who serve in what's commonly recognized as *the five-fold ministry* (apostle, prophet, evangelist, pastor, and teacher). It is extremely important because it is through this *power* that we're able to **"heal the sick, cleanse the diseased, raise the dead, (and) cast out devils" (Matthew 10:8)**.

As ministers of the Gospel we also need the power of God in order to minister *effectively* to people and help meet their other spiritual needs. Ministering to people is about much more than sharing the Word, counseling, advising, praying for people, and encouraging them. Ministering to people is also about being able to employ the power of God in healing from sickness and disease, raising the dead, casting out devils, and performing any other type of miracle God is capable and desiring to perform through us as ministers of the Gospel of God and ministers of the power of God! But the power and the ability to operate in the supernatural <u>only</u> come by way of being filled with the Holy Spirit.

CALLED TO SAVE, SERVE, AND MEET MANY NEEDS

If we have been called to serve as an undershepherd (pastor) of God's flock, a part of our responsibility is tending to the supernatural needs of the sheep, or would-be sheep. There are people in churches everywhere who are being attacked with sickness, disease, physical ailments, and different types of demonic harassment or possession. And if the shepherd who has been called to care for them has not been equipped or **"endued with power" (Luke 24:49)** to care for them, the sheep will be forced to live with sickness, disease, demonic torment, or some other deeds of the devil.

Sometimes Christians even die prematurely due to sickness or disease that the power of God through Holy Spirit baptism could heal them from. But this requires people to recognize that they are without this power and seek to possess it, or to have faith once they are in possession of that power.

It pains me to hear pastors, ministers, or church members say they have never been a part of, seen, or heard of anyone in their church receive supernatural healing. It's not because most pastors don't believe in supernatural healing; it's that they don't have the power to operate in supernatural healing. Most pastors believe in supernatural healing but have ceased laying hands on parishioners and believing for healing because when they did, no one ever got healed. So, in discouragement, and in fear of people questioning their calling, their access to power, or the realness of God's power, they've simply resorted to praying *for* people from a distance, instead of praying for people on the spot.

KEEP PRAYING, PASTOR

Before I continue, I want to acknowledge that there are many pastors who are in fact filled with the Holy Spirit (according to the teaching of the Scriptures) and have prayed for people to receive healing, but many of them have remained ill. The pastor then stopped praying for healing altogether because he feared the message that was being sent to others when those he prayed for did not receive healing. But it is important to say *to* every pastor who has stopped praying for healing for this reason, and *on behalf* of these pastors, that people not receiving healing is not always because the pastor does not have the power of the Holy Spirit or is not anointed to heal.

Sure, if a pastor has unrepentant sin (transgression or iniquity) in their life, it will definitely hinder their ability to minister in the power of the Holy Spirit, even if they are filled with the Holy Spirit. This could indeed be a reason why those who were prayed for were not healed. But also, and more often than not, the absence of healing is a product of what's going on with the person and not the pastor. Sometimes, according to the Scriptures, healing may not take place if it is the work of God designed to discipline His child in an effort to get them back on the obedience track. This may not be popular but it's scriptural.

**You should know in your heart that as a
man chastens his son, so the Lord
your God chastens you.
Deuteronomy 8:5**

**And you have forgotten the exhortation
which speaks to you as to sons:
"My son, do not despise the chastening
of the Lord, nor be discouraged when
you are rebuked by Him; ⁶ For whom
the Lord loves He chastens, and scourges
every son whom He receives." ⁷ If you
endure chastening, God deals with you
as with sons; for what son is there whom
a father does not chasten?
Hebrews 12:5-7**

Throughout the Bible we see sickness and disease being a product of sin and disobedience. Sometimes sickness or disease was caused and constructively used by God. But sometimes it was the natural consequence of any different type of sin—from disobedience, to unforgiveness, to having a hateful heart, etc. But the point is, sometimes people don't receive healing in their body because of the presence and ongoing practice of sin in their life and not because the pastor, minister, elder, etc., isn't empowered by God to heal. And sometimes healing is delayed for reasons unbeknownst to the pastor or the person.

In any instance, I would encourage pastors and others who have stopped praying for healing to resume praying and believing God for healing. Explain that the absence of healing doesn't mean God can't heal, doesn't want to heal, or that you as the pastor or other church leaders aren't empowered to heal, but that there may be obstacles elsewhere. In resuming praying for healing, even if only one person out of five receives healing, that one person is worth weathering the speculation of why others were not healed.

And that one healing may provide the testimony that provided the faith needed by others to help them receive their healing.

> **If My people who are called by My name**
> **will humble themselves, and pray and seek**
> **My face, <u>and turn from their wicked ways</u>,**
> **then will I hear from heaven, and will**
> **forgive their sin and <u>heal</u> their land.**

Some churches are so large that the senior pastor couldn't possibly pray for every person who needs healing. But the power of Holy Spirit baptism operates in and through assistant pastors, associates pastors, ministers, elders, presbyters, teachers, deacons, and lay members as well. We don't have to have the spiritual gift of healing in order for God to heal others through us. We only need to be *filled* with the Holy Spirit in order to exercise the power of the Holy Spirit!

But this power is not at our disposal simply because we're saved or because we have been called into the ministry. We need to be filled with the Holy Spirit in order to possess and operate in the power of the Holy Spirit.

> **The absence of healing**
> **doesn't mean God can't heal,**
> **doesn't want to heal, or that**
> **leaders are not empowered to heal.**

SAMARITANS SAVED BUT NOT
FILLED AT THE TIME OF SALVATION

The first scriptural example of Christians being saved without yet being baptized *by* Jesus with the Holy Spirit is found in **Acts 8:5** when **"Philip went down to the city of Samaria and preached Christ to them."**

> **But when they believed Philip as he preached the things concerning the kingdom of God and the name of Jesus Christ, both men and women were baptized.**
> **Acts 8:12**

> **Now when the apostles who were at Jerusalem heard that Samaria had received the Word of God, they sent Peter and John to them, [15] who, when they had come down, prayed for them that they might receive the Holy Spirit. [16] For as yet He had fallen upon none of them. They had only been baptized in the name of the Lord Jesus. [17] Then (Peter and John) laid hands on them, and they received the Holy Spirit.**
> **Acts 8:14-17**

There is a great deal of *good stuff* in this particular story about the Samaritans being saved and being filled with the Holy Spirit.

The first thing I want to point out is that after Philip shared the Gospel and they believed in Jesus, the Samaritans were saved. The very next thing Philip did was baptize them in water. After that, the apostles received word in Jerusalem that the Samaritans had received the witness about Jesus as it had been prophetically instructed in

Acts 1:8, **"Ye shall be witnesses unto Me in Jerusalem, and all Judea and <u>Samaria</u>, and to the end of the earth."** Upon learning this it was decided that Peter and John would travel to Samaria to minister Holy Spirit baptism to the new converts because the Holy Spirit **"had fallen upon none of them."**

*(It's noteworthy that Philip was unable to lead them to being filled with the Holy Spirit, but it took Peter and John who were apostles to come and do so. This says to us that not everyone who is called to the Word ministry or is empowered by the Spirit to do **"miracles and signs"** can lead others to Holy Spirit baptism. It is seemingly a specialty ministry. And even those who are called to operate in this capacity should receive training on how to do so effectively.)*

Jerusalem was approximately thirty-five to forty miles north of Samaria, which was at least one day's journey, possibly longer depending on the mode of transportation and other relevant factors like rest stops, unscheduled ministry requirements, or perhaps the need to travel discreetly to avoid the fate that had recently befallen Stephen at the hand of Saul and others who were persecuting Christians. But assuming Peter and John were able to make the one-day trek in one day, it still means the Samaritans had been saved one day *without* yet being filled until the two apostles arrived, **"laid hands on them, and they received the Holy Spirit."** The point is, this serves as evidence that it's possible to be saved and *not yet* filled with the Holy Spirit.

Also in this historical account of Holy Spirit baptism performed *by* Jesus, we find that the other two baptisms are present. Verses 12 and 16 talk about their water baptism, probably *by* Philip; but of course the baptism *by* the Holy Spirit invisibly took place as well, in the moment they **"believed Philip as he preached the things concerning the kingdom of God and the name of Jesus Christ."** Remember, in the very instant a person receives Jesus in their heart by faith, the Holy Spirit baptizes them into the body of Christ, making them children of El-Elyon, the Most High God!

> "...prayed for them
> that they might receive
> the Holy Spirit. For as yet He
> had fallen upon none of them..."

SAUL SAVED BUT NOT
FILLED AT THE TIME OF SALVATION

Another example of a person having received Jesus as their Savior but not immediately being filled with the Holy Spirit is Saul (before his name was changed to Paul). The following took place not long after his role in the death of Stephen, while Saul was seeking the demise of more of those who followed the Way.

> **Then Saul, still breathing threats and murder
> against the disciples of the Lord, went to the
> high priest [2] and asked letters from him to the
> synagogues of Damascus, so that if he found any
> who were of the Way, whether men or women, he
> might bring them bound to Jerusalem. [3] As he
> journeyed he came near Damascus, and suddenly
> a light shone around him from heaven. [4] The he fell
> to the ground, and heard a voice saying to him, "Saul,
> Saul, why are you persecuting Me?" [5] And he said,
> "Where are You, Lord?" The Lord said, "I am Jesus,
> whom you are persecuting. It is hard for you to kick
> against the goads." [6] So he, trembling and astonished
> said, "Lord, what do You want me to do?" The Lord
> said to him, "Arise and go into the city and you
> will be told what you must do."**
> **Acts 9:1-6**

Saul accepted Jesus as Savior and received salvation in the moment reflected in verse 6 when he realized Jesus had been resurrected from the dead and was speaking to him while on his way to arrest other Christians. (*It was also in this moment that Saul was baptized by the Holy Spirit and placed into the body of Christ as a child of God.*)

When Saul heard the voice of Jesus he immediately surrendered and submitted his life to Him in asking, *"Lord, what will You have me to do?"* This was the place and the point of the apostle Paul's conversion and salvation. However, we find no mention of him being filled with the Holy Spirit at this time. We don't see Saul being filled with the Holy Spirit until a short time later.

In following the instructions of Jesus to **"go into the city,"** Saul journeyed three days without sight, food, or water to the house of Judas (not the one who betrayed Jesus), which was in Damascus.

During this time, the Lord had a conversation with Ananias about Saul and what He had planned for him and how He wanted Ananias to help. After a time of justifiable skepticism because of what he had *"heard from many about (Saul), and how much harm he has done to Your saints in Jerusalem,"* Ananias gave in to the trustworthy urging of the Lord.

"And Ananias went his way and entered the house; and laying his hands on him he said, 'Brother Saul, the Lord Jesus, who appeared to you on the road as you came, has sent me that you may receive your sight and <u>be filled with the Holy Spirit.</u>' "
Acts 9:17

What we find here is that it was at least three days after Saul had a soul-saving encounter with Jesus on the road to Damascus that he received the filling of the Holy Spirit. This means Saul was saved for a short period of time without having been *filled* with the Holy Spirit.

> **It is possible to be saved**
> **but not yet filled;**
> **but it is impossible to be**
> **filled if we're not yet saved.**

K. SHELDON SAVED BUT NOT
FILLED AT THE TIME OF SALVATION

My personal experience was receiving Holy Spirit baptism after having committed my life to Christ. Through repentance from sin and faith in Jesus, I gave my life to the Lord on October 23, 1988. On this same day the Holy Spirit indwelt me and I was <u>baptized</u> *by* Him and placed into the family of God. I was <u>baptized</u> in water *by* Pastor Samuel Craig, Jr., the assistant pastor of my church, on November 6, 1988. However, I wasn't filled, or <u>baptized</u> *by* Jesus with the Holy Spirit, until a few months later. When it happened, I didn't exactly know what had taken place because I had not been taught anything about being filled with the Spirit in the short time I had been walking with God. *(I will share more about my encounter in a later chapter.)*

Unless a person is a part of a church that recognizes that not everyone who gives their life to Christ is filled with the Holy Spirit in that moment, they may go a long time, or even a lifetime, without ever being filled.

However, there are many churches that give an invitation for Holy Spirit baptism at or around the time they give an invitation for people to receive Jesus. Though not everyone may be ready to take that step (coming to Christ was a big enough step for them, and they may need to just take it one step at a time, which is fine), others will be open to hearing about it, trusting in what they hear, and willing to be filled at that time.

Some churches provide a Holy Spirit baptism class, or classes, wherein they teach people on the subject and invite them to be filled with the Holy Spirit at the end of the session(s). This approach is designed to provide more in-depth teaching than the abbreviated explanation given after one accepts the invitation to be filled.

Either way is okay. But of course, the more one learns about a subject, the fewer obstacles of confusion and misunderstanding they will have to overcome on the path of being filled. That is not to say that people *must* have some teaching in order to be filled because sometimes people get filled without having had anything explained to them, or without having any prior knowledge or understanding of what happened to them once they've been filled. This was my experience. I had not been taught, nor had I even heard of anyone talk about Holy Spirit baptism as it relates to tongues.

But, whether it's through an abbreviated explanation of Holy Spirit baptism, a class, or a series of classes, many people who have been saved for moments, days, weeks, months, or years, come to be filled upon realizing that, though they have been saved, they have not been *filled.* That's perfectly fine, and nothing to be ashamed of.

DISCIPLES SAVED BUT NOT
FILLED AT THE SAME TIME

One final account of Christians being saved at one point and being filled with the Holy Spirit sometime later is found during the ministry of the apostle while in the city of Ephesus. Let's take a look.

**And it happened, while Apollos was at
Corinth, that Paul, having passed through
the upper regions, came to Ephesus.
And finding some disciples
[2] he said to them, "<u>Did you receive the
Holy Spirit when you believed?</u>" So they
said to him, "We have not so much as heard**

> whether there is a Holy Spirit." ³ And he said
> to them, "Into what then were your baptized?"
> So they said, "Into John's baptism."
> ⁴ Then Paul said, "John indeed baptized with
> a baptism of repentance, saying to the people that
> they should believe on Him who would come
> after him, that is, on Christ Jesus."
> ⁵ When they heard this, they were
> baptized in the name of the Lord Jesus.
> ⁶ And when Paul had laid hands on them,
> the Holy Spirit came upon them, and they
> spoke with tongues and prophesied.
> Acts 19:1-6

There are a number of things to understand and consider about this passage. The first thing is, the fact that the Bible refers to these gentlemen Paul encountered as *"disciples"* means they were already saved. The stated fact that they *"believed"* (in Jesus through the ministry of John the Baptist) also acts as evidence that they were saved.

For the point we are seeking to make about how it is possible to be saved and not yet filled with the Holy Spirit, it is also important to state that **Acts 19** takes place over twenty years after these *"disciples"* had come to know Jesus through the ministry of John the Baptist. It is also key to note that it had been over seventeen years since the Holy Spirit first filled believers in Acts chapter 2, which means that these *"disciples"* had been saved for nearly two decades without having been filled with the Holy Spirit. They had experienced almost twenty years of the Spirit's dwelling, but not of the Spirit's filling.

The fact that we plainly see this in the Bible allows us to know that it is not an uncommon thing for Christians to be saved for long periods of time but not yet be filled. It's not a negative thing or an indictment of one's salvation or spiritual maturity. Neither is it anything to be ashamed of. It is not uncommon for Christians to have not had these truths of the Bible brought to their attention.

WHY ASK?

Another interesting point to consider about Paul's encounter with these **"disciples"** is, since they **"believed"** and were saved through the ministry of John the Baptist, they had already been baptized *by* the Holy Spirit, or placed into the family of God. Of course, Paul would have understood this. And it was with this understanding that he asked them, **"Did you receive the Holy Spirit when you believed?"** He asked them this because he knew they were two separate things.

Think about it…if being baptized *by* the Holy Spirit was the same as **"receiving"** or being baptized *in* the Holy Spirit, Paul would not have continued the dialogue with them about having received the Holy Spirit after learning about their salvation. After they said, **"into John's baptism,"** Paul continued because he knew John's message led them to Jesus, baptism *by* the Holy Spirit, and water baptism *by* John, but not baptism *in* the Holy Spirit *by* Jesus.

In like manner, if receiving the baptism of the Holy Spirit *by* Jesus was an automatic occurrence for everyone who was saved, this *living Word* question, **"Have you received the Holy Spirit since you believed?"** would not be in the Bible because it would be a foregone conclusion by virtue of a Christian's saving belief in Jesus.

The apostle Paul was inspired by the Holy Spirit to ask these heirs of salvation if they had received the Holy Spirit because he understood that it was possible for them to have been saved disciples who had received Jesus but had not yet received or been filled with the Holy Spirit. As was the case with those disciples back then, so is the case with us as disciples today. Thousands have received Jesus, but have not yet received the baptism of the Holy Spirit. Undoubtedly, they are saved, but not yet filled.

> **Nearly twenty years of dwelling,
> but no Holy Spirit filling.**

THE HIGHWAY OF HUMILITY

I love the heart of these disciples. It wasn't haughty; it was humble. The humility they demonstrated when they learned that there was something about *"receiving the Holy Spirit"* that they had yet to be taught was honorable, refreshing, and Christ-like. In the nearly twenty-five years that I've been teaching on Holy Spirit baptism and the various countries I've taught it in, every now and then I come across Christians who get quite perturbed at the idea that there is something about Holy Spirit baptism they don't know or fully understand. But it has been my experience that a large majority of Christians are open to considering perspectives they have not been introduced to. In fairness, I must also say that many of those whose initial reaction is one of agitation at the notion of not knowing it all are humbled when the Holy Spirit opens their mind and reveals to them what they had not previously understood. And far more often than not, they receive the gift of the Holy Spirit at the invitation.

After Paul, who had been saved a shorter period time than each of them, offered a brief explanation of why they were not yet filled, we don't find them huffing and puffing and talking about how they had been saved for over twenty years, or acting like they already had all they needed to have, or knew all they needed to know. Instead, we find them receiving what Paul told them and then receiving the Holy Spirit Who filled them!

Nothing reveals humility like the willingness to consider (or reconsider) biblical truths that we have overlooked or not yet been taught. And when we humble ourselves and receive such truths, we position ourselves to receive that which God wants to increase us through.

DON'T BE A KNOW-IT-ALL

I have long said, *"None of us know all there is to know, about what we know."* Simply put, it doesn't matter how much we know about a subject, there's more to learn and know about that subject.

The first time I taught Holy Spirit baptism it was a one- or two-part series. The next time I taught it, it was a four-part series. The time after that, it was a six-part series. The final time I taught a series on Holy Spirit baptism it had become a ten-and-a-half-part series *(I know, I know…how did I come up with half of a part. I'm not sure. I think I was just trying to squeeze out as much paste from the tube as I could!)* Since that time I have added a two-part addendum for pastors and those who are called to minister Holy Spirit baptism to others. But the point is, although I knew some things about Holy Spirit baptism when I taught the subject the first, second, and third times, I didn't know all there was to know about it. Had I thought so and stopped studying and looking for more insight, I would have kept myself from learning more about a subject that has been a blessing to countless people throughout the world.

> **None of us know all there is to know,**
> **about what we know.**
> **If we allow ourselves to know more,**
> **we position ourselves to grow more!**

In the many countries (and churches) that I have taught and ministered Holy Spirit baptism in, it never fails that people learn something they never knew. Many people who have been in church for a long time (including pastors) get filled with the Holy Spirit after being shown truths they had never seen or been taught.

In Pakistan, India, and countries in Africa where I hold seminars or pastors' conferences and teach Holy Spirit baptism, I already know that those seminars and conferences are attended by pastors and people from varying denominations that have different understandings and beliefs of this subject. But it never fails, *every single time* I teach Holy Spirit baptism, nearly every single person that is present, pastors included, receive the teaching, and at the invitation to be baptized *by* Jesus, they also receive the filling of the Holy Spirit.

This is because they trust what they see in God's Word, and they're not willing to allow the position of their domination to be an idol that trumps the truth of what the Bible makes plain to them.

A LONG TIME COMING

I recall being invited to minister at a church in America and teaching Holy Spirit baptism. After the message, I gave an invitation for people to come and receive the filling of the Holy Spirit. Initially, as is commonly the case, no one moved from their seat. But I had learned to be patient because there *must have* been people there who needed to be filled or the Lord would not have led me to teach that subject and bid people to come and receive.

After a moment or two, one person stood up and came forward. Then another, and another, and another! Shortly thereafter, the altar area was nearly full with people who had come forward to be *filled* with the Holy Spirit!

After walking them through the process which included instructions, expectations, how to silently respond to doubt that may visit their mind in that moment, the prayer of salvation, and a prayer *asking* God to *give* them the Holy Spirit—it happened (like it always does), ***"they were all filled with the Holy Spirit and began to speak with other tongues."***

After a few minutes of basking in the presence of God and simmering in the glory of His Spirit, a number of people were teary-eyed. Some were smiling from ear to ear, and *all* were filled—not just with the Holy Spirit, but also with the joy of the Lord!

After the service ended, I was greeting and hugging people and taking pictures when a gentleman who had been filled during the service approached me with tears in his eyes and said, *"Thank you! I have been wanting to receive the Holy Spirit for fifteen years!"*

Needless to say, that blessed me! It didn't surprise me, but it blessed me. It blessed me not just because he had been filled with the Holy Spirit or because he was a leader in the church, but because as a church leader and a seasoned Christian he was still humble enough to receive truths from the Scriptures he had never seen before. And because he was willing to come forward to be filled without being concerned what others around him may have thought about it, or him. That's humility that pays dividends!

What allowed that church leader to receive the *filling* of the Holy Spirit after fifteen years of desiring it was his humility, and the understanding he received from the Scriptures. It was his ability to comprehend and make sense of biblical truths that brought clarity and order where there was previously chaos and confusion. The keys of clarity and understanding of the Word *rightly divided* freed him to experience that which had long eluded him.

This is an example of what Jesus meant when He said, ***"And you shall know <u>the truth</u>, and <u>the truth</u> shall make you free."***

Christians all over the world from varying denominations are rediscovering Holy Spirit baptism!

THE UNCOMMON INSTANT OCCURRENCE

As I stated earlier in this chapter, there are times when people receive the filling, or the baptism of the Holy Spirit, at the time they receive Jesus as their Savior. **Acts 10** shows us the only clear-cut example of this occurring.

It took place after the Lord sent Peter and a few men *(though not named, at least two of them were with Peter when he was Spirit filled on the Day of Pentecost in Acts chapter 2)* to share the good news about Jesus with a fellow named Cornelius and a group of family and friends who had gathered at his house awaiting Peter's arrival. What happened next was nothing short of miraculous!

> **"While Peter was still speaking these words, the Holy Spirit fell upon all those who heard the Word. ⁴⁵ And those of the circumcision who believed were astonished, as many as came with Peter, because the gift of the Holy Spirit had been poured out on the Gentiles also. ⁴⁶ For they heard them speak with tongues and magnify God. Then Peter answered, ⁴⁷ "Can anyone forbid water, that these should not be baptized who have received the Holy Spirit just as we have?"**
> **Acts 10:44-47**

When Cornelius and his friends and family heard the message about Jesus, they believed it. And their belief led to their salvation. Though unseen and unmentioned in the story, the very first thing to take place in that moment was their baptism *by* the Holy Spirit into the body of Christ (or the family of God). Next, they were baptized *by* Jesus *in* the Holy Spirit—indicated by them speaking in tongues.

This is clear evidence that sometimes a person can be filled with the Holy Spirit at the time they trust in Jesus for their salvation. Though this seems to be the exception more than the rule, it is a possibility, nevertheless. In the meetings I hold in various countries (whether I'm teaching on Holy Spirit baptism or another subject), following an invitation for people to pray and confess their faith in Jesus, after a brief explanation, I always extend an invitation for people to also pray to be baptized in the Holy Spirit. And praise God, people always respond to both invitations.

Many of the people who respond to the invitation to be baptized by Jesus with the Holy Spirit have just moments before expressed their faith in Jesus as Savior. But in even rarer instances, as was the case with Cornelius' house, people can be filled instantly upon receiving Jesus. However, there are always many who respond only to the invitation to be baptized in the Holy Spirit because they have had a saving relationship with Jesus a very long time. Nevertheless, in their humility they come recognizing there is something else that God has to help and bless them in their relationship with Him. They want it! And they receive it!

BETTER LATER THAN NEVER

When a person receives the baptism of the Holy Spirit isn't as important as a person receiving it at some point. Sure, the sooner the better. But better later than never! Receiving it early is good because it allows one to enjoy the benefits of being filled while they're young in Christ. Receiving it later is okay too, because it can revitalize a person's relationship with the Lord and rejuvenate their area(s) of service or ministry. It may also launch people into a new ministry or a new level of ministry effectiveness!

But the point is, we can be *filled* with the Holy Spirit at any stage of our relationship with God, be it after a few minutes, days, weeks, months, or decades! *When* we receive it is not the most important thing; *that* we receive it, is!

SAME THING

I want to take a moment and make the case for *Holy Spirit baptism,* the *filling Holy Spirit,* and *receiving the Holy Spirit* all being one in the same thing. First, let's look again at the Words of Jesus in **Acts 1:5**.

> **"...for John truly baptized with water,
> but you shall be <u>baptized with the Holy
> Spirit</u> not many days from now.**

The "not many days from now" was a reference to the Day of Pentecost. Let's look again at what took place on this day of promise and see how it's worded.

> **When the Day of Pentecost had fully come,
> they were all with one accord in one place.
> Acts 2:1**

> **Acts 2:4
> And they were all <u>filled with the Holy Spirit</u>
> and began to speak with other tongues,
> as the Spirit gave them utterance.**

In **Acts 2:4** we find the fulfillment of what Jesus promised in **Acts 1:5**. Notice how Jesus used the term **"baptized with the Holy Spirit"** when the promise was given in **Acts 1:5**, but when the promise was fulfilled we find the term, **"filled with the Holy Spirit"** in **Acts 2:4**. Although two different terms are used, they are clearly the same event.

This next piece of evidence that *filled* and *baptized* with the Holy Spirit are not different occurrences but are one and the same thing takes us back to Family and Friends Day at Cornelius' home, when Peter was the guest speaker. Please look again at **Acts 10:46-47**.

> **"For (or because) they heard them
> speak with tongues and magnify God.
> Then Peter answered, "Can anyone forbid water,
> that these should not be baptized who have
> <u>received the Holy Spirit</u> just as we have?"**

While Peter was explaining to the apostles and others who were in Judea why he went, preached the Gospel, and broke bread with non-Jews (which was not considered acceptable by them to do so), Peter told them how **"the Holy Spirit fell upon them, as upon us at the beginning."** Of course he was talking about when they **"received the Holy Spirit."** And then Peter says this in **Acts 11:16**:

> **"Then I remembered the Word of the Lord,**
> **how He said, 'John indeed baptized with**
> **water, but you shall be <u>baptized with</u>**
> **<u>the Holy Spirit</u>.' "**

Notice, Peter equated what had happened with the Gentiles **"<u>receiving the Holy Spirit</u>"** with what happened to them on the Day of Pentecost when they were **"<u>filled with the Holy Spirit</u>"** and what Jesus promised during His final time with them, **"you shall be <u>baptized with the Holy Spirit</u>."** Positively, being baptized, filled, and receiving the Holy Spirit are all the exact same thing.

So, if you have yet to *receive*, be *baptized*, or *filled* with the Holy Spirit, what's the holdup? Go to God; He wants you to receive! He wants to baptize you! He's wants to fill you with His power!

CHAPTER 4

TONGUES, TONGUES, TONGUES!

PART 1 – WHAT IS THE BIG DEAL ABOUT TONGUES?

And they were all filled with the Holy Spirit
and began to speak with other tongues,
as the Spirit gave them utterance.
Acts 2:4

I would be surprised if there is a more controversial element of
Holy Spirit baptism than that of speaking in tongues.

For centuries, there has been a confusion, uncertainty, and
misunderstanding about tongues in general and about whether
or not tongues plays a role in Holy Spirit baptism. Many hold
the position that tongues are merely one of the gifts of the Holy
Spirit—a gift that not everyone has; while others claim the use of
tongues and need for tongues have both passed away.

Before I continue on in this thought I think it is important to
address the faulty assertion offered by some that *tongues have passed
away"* or *"they are no longer used, useful, or needed."* First of all, *"these
times"* are the *same times* in which tongues was introduced, which is
the era of the New Testament church. The New Testament church
was birthed on the Day of Pentecost when both the Holy Spirit
came, filled, and enabled believers in Christ to speak in tongues.

It was also on that day that the apostle Peter delivered the very first post-ascension Gospel message about the life, death, burial, and resurrection of Jesus. Also, the birthday of the New Testament church shared the new-birthday of three thousand souls who were added to those who were already followers of the Christ. *Those times* were the times of preaching the Gospel, leading the lost to salvation, fellowshipping, and breaking bread with fellow saints in the faith. In *these times* we're doing the same things because *these times* are *those times*. Therefore, if speaking in tongues was for *those times* and *these times* are *those times,* we are still in the era for which tongues were enabled.

Secondly, the notion that tongues *"are no longer used"* is not accurate because literally thousands and thousands (if not millions) of people all over the world still speak in tongues. I know this for a fact because I have ministered Holy Spirit baptism in a number of countries and have seen people speaking in tongues. They could not do so if tongues were passed away or were no longer being used.

Thirdly, as far as the idea that tongues *"are no longer useful or needed,"* I would say, as long as the purposes for which tongues were given are still in existence, tongues *must* still be in operation in order to fulfill those purposes. *(We will address these purposes in great detail later in this section.)* Saying tongues are no longer *"useful or needed"* in *"these times"* is like saying we no longer have need for doctors, beds, or auto technicians. As long as people get sick, sleep, or have slipping transmissions, we are going to need doctors, beds, and auto technicians.

In the same way, as long as we have the needs that tongues are designed to meet, there will always be tongues in the era of the New Testament Christian church.

UNTIL THEN, MY FRIEND

Some have been caused to think that tongues are no longer relevant by a passage in **1 Corinthians 13:8** which says:

**Love never fails. But whether
there are prophecies, they will fail;
whether there are <u>tongues, they
will cease</u>; whether there is
knowledge it will vanish away.**

The first point I'll make in refuting this verse as evidence to the supposition that tongues are no longer in existence is the word, "will". The word "will" speaks of a future occurrence, or the coming of a time when a particular something is to take place. For example, if I say, *"I <u>will</u> go to the store,"* one will deduce from that statement that I am not currently at the store, but plan to be at some future time. In like fashion, when the apostle Paul writes that tongues **"<u>will</u> cease"** he is speaking of that which will take place in a future age when the affairs of Christianity on earth come to an end. We know that the business of Christianity and God's Kingdom on the earth will not end until the return of Christ the King.

In verse 10, Paul helps me to solidify this fact by stating, **"When that which is perfect has come, then that which is in part will be done away."** I believe, and it is widely held by many scholars and theologians, that this is a reference to the Second Coming of Christ. This is simply because Jesus is "perfect" and Jesus has promised to "come" again. So, when He, **"that which is perfect has come"** on His second return, **"then that which is in part will be done away,"** and then **"tongues...will cease."** However, until then, tongues still exist to fulfill their meaningful purpose.

The second point of refute from **1 Corinthians 10:8** I'd like to make is a simple one...if **"knowledge"** has not **"vanished"** (and it hasn't), neither then can **"tongues"** have **"ceased."**

**As long as the purpose
for tongues still exist,
tongues must still exist.**

Another reason for opposition to tongues and their role in Holy Spirit baptism, a reason that should not be overlooked or taken lightly, is that of false teachers. False teachers don't oppose everything that's true (or else they couldn't pass themselves off as true teachers), just certain things. Considering the fact that false teachers are plants from the kingdom of the enemy, and Holy Spirit baptism and tongues is a threat to his kingdom, it's no wonder that false teachers would oppose the biblical doctrine of Holy Spirit baptism and its accompanying tongues.

I am not suggesting that everyone who opposes Holy Spirit baptism with tongues as its manifestation is a false teacher. That is most certainly not the case. There are many God-fearing, God-loving, and people-loving ministers and pastors who oppose this doctrine but are genuinely called by God and do a good job in ministry. But undoubtedly there are many false teachers in the world and in the church who oppose this teaching because of how great of a threat it is to the many-fold agenda of the enemy of our soul.

We don't teach or talk much about false teachers, at least not in America. But I think we should because when the issue of false teachers goes unaddressed, the doctrine of false teachers goes unchecked. And whatever goes unchecked is free to deceive and spiritually damage people.

> **But there were also false apostles among the people, even as <u>there will be false teachers among you,</u> who will secretly bring in destructive heresies, even denying the Lord who brought them, and bring on themselves swift destruction. [2] And many will follow their destructive ways, because of whom the <u>way of truth will be blasphemed.</u>**
> **2 Peter 2:1-2**

BAFFLING

Outside of the obvious reasoning of false teachers' opposition to tongues, others, for other reasons, are oddly and starkly opposed to tongues. I find their resistance somewhat baffling when I consider the fact that every one of the New Testament writers spoke in tongues. It's baffling because every day we read their writings and encourage others to read their writings, we use their writings to study, preach, and teach from, and we acknowledge that their writings were **"given by inspiration of God."** But yet we are against tongues that were spoken by these great men of God who have been a blessing to us and to millions and millions of Christians all over the world.

That's baffling to say the least. How is it that Christians trust in the writings of Matthew, Mark, Luke, John, Paul, Timothy, Titus, Peter, and James, who spoke in tongues, but are themselves against speaking in tongues? And how is it that some Christians can be adamantly against that which is *clearly* from God and a work of His Holy Spirit Whom He sent to be our *Helper*? *(Selah)*

A part of the opposition to tongues for many, now and down through history, stems from the fact that they believed in Holy Spirit baptism and the evidence of speaking in tongues and sought to be filled according to that biblically prescribed pattern. But when they were not filled *(for whatever reason, be it they were unsaved at the time they sought to be filled, unbelieving that they could or would be filled, or they were impatient and discouraged because it didn't happen right away)*, they began to set themselves against tongues and it being the evidence of being filled with the Holy Spirit.

This has even been the case for the founders of certain Christian denominations. Because they could not or did not speak in tongues, the denomination was established in being anti-tongues in its doctrine. This doctrinal posture was taught to its leaders and followers and has been passed down through the generations of their denomination. And even spin-off churches who claim to be nondenominational but have been heavily indoctrinated through their denominational association teach opposition to tongues because the anti-tongues fruit of their learning bears seed that brings forth fruit after its own kind.

The denominational influence of opposing tongues is responsible for **"making the Word of God of no effect through traditions which have been handed down" (Mark 7:13).** Consequently, many Christians are more trusting of man's doctrine and traditional beliefs than God's inerrant Word. But the Lord is looking for men and women who love and trust Him and His Word more than their denomination and its anti-tongues doctrine. And when He finds such men and women, He will show Himself strong on their behalf!

> **"(They) are nullifying and making void the Word of God through tradition, which (they) in turn hand down. And many things of this kind are (they) doing."**

As we will discover later in this chapter and in the following chapter, tongues are extremely helpful to the individual Christian and the body of Christ as a whole. As such, I have come to believe that the harsh opposition and disdain for tongues held by some is itself a work of opposition forces who aim to keep as many Christians as possible from utilizing that which is a tremendous blessing for the children of the light, and a damaging force to the kingdom of darkness!

DEMONIC?

I have even heard it said that tongues are of the devil. This of course cannot be true. Because tongues accompanied the baptism of the Holy Spirit on the Day of Pentecost, it means that the Holy Spirit is the cause for the occurrence of tongues and our ability to speak in them. For anyone to say or suggest tongues are *of the* devil, they are being disrespectful to the Holy Spirit of God at the very least, and possibly blasphemous. The Bible reveals one aspect of blasphemy to be, attributing anything that is of the Holy Spirit to the devil.

> **Now when the Pharisees heard**
> **(that Jesus had cast out a demon)**
> **the said, "This fellow does not cast**
> **out demons except by Beelzebub,**
> **the ruler of demons."**
> **Matthew 12:24**

Consider the response of the Christ:

> **But if I cast out demons by the**
> **Spirit of God, surely the kingdom**
> **of God has come upon you.**
> **Matthew 12:28**

> **Therefore, I say to you, every sin**
> **and blasphemy will be forgiven men,**
> **but the blasphemy against the Spirit**
> **will not be forgiven men.**
> **Matthew 12:31**

Clearly Jesus is saying that attributing anything that is done **"by the Spirit of God"** to the **"ruler of demons"** (the devil) is blasphemy. This is exactly what is taking place when people say tongues is of the devil when the Scriptures clearly reveal that tongues, *sign and gift*, are works of the Holy Spirit.

The untruth that tongues is of the devil is designed to keep Christians from desiring to speak in tongues because no Christian wants a part of anything that is of the devil. Oddly enough, buying into the lie and therefore *not* wanting to speak in tongues is us being a part of something that is of the devil…his deception.

The fact that the devil lies in seeking to keep Christians away from spiritual truths isn't new. In fact, it's more than a notion; it's a proven reality. We know that the devil can get into the mind of good men and women of God and cause them to aggressively deny and vehemently oppose spiritual truths because this is exactly what the devil did to Peter.

> **From that time Jesus began to show to His disciples that He must go to Jerusalem, and suffer many things from the elders and chief priests and scribes, and be killed, and be raised the third day. ²² Then Peter took Him aside and began to rebuke Him, saying, "Far be it from You, Lord; this shall not happen to You!" ²³ But (Jesus) turned and said to Peter, "Get behind Me, Satan! You are an offense to Me, for you are not mindful of the things of God, but the things of man."**
> **Matthew 16:21-23**

Although Jesus turned and spoke to Peter, the Lord's rebuff was intended for the devil who caused Peter to stand in verbal aggression against the truth Jesus shared about His pending death and resurrection. What the devil did with Peter is often what is happening when good men and women of God oppose the truths concerning Holy Spirit baptism and all the Bible reveals about it.

If the devil was able to do this to Peter, the leader of the disciples who literally walked with Jesus, learned directly from the lips of Jesus, and was an eyewitness to all the Christ did, any man or woman of God today can also be adamantly set against truth. I have seen people respond to the mention and sound teaching of tongues with a hostile nastiness I knew wasn't from God—just as Jesus knew Peter's response to the truth He shared wasn't from God.

To understand why the devil rises up even in children of God in opposition of certain truths, we have to look closely and carefully consider the situation between Jesus and Peter wherein the devil interjected. Jesus was sharing with Peter about His soon-coming death and resurrection. If He had simply stopped at telling Peter about His death the devil would have remained silent, finding no need to offer opposition. But because Jesus also mentioned His resurrection, that which would defeat death, which the devil was supportive of, Satan lost it and used Peter to "rebuke" Jesus.

(If Jesus had not been discerning of who was speaking through Peter, instead of a rebuke, Peter may have had an intimate encounter with a lightning bolt! Praise God for discernment…and mercy!)

The devil rose up in opposition to the mentioning and the truth of the resurrection of Jesus because he knew the resurrection of the Christ would deal a severe blow to the kingdom of darkness. It is for this same reason that the devil sometimes raises up in men and women of God at the mention of tongues, or even when sound, biblical teaching of Holy Spirit baptism is presented. Holy Spirit baptism and all of its elements *(tongues, the miracle-working power of healing and miracles, the anointing that destroys yokes, the manifestation of certain spiritual gifts, the effective operation in other spiritual gifts, accelerated spiritual growth, etc.)* are mighty weapons of God against the devil's kingdom; weapons he doesn't want Christians to be in possession of for obvious reasons.

TRUTH: THE GREATEST THREAT TO DARKNESS

Because the topic of tongues generates so many questions and has caused so much chaos and division in the body of Christ, I thought it would be a good idea to tackle this issue by looking closely at the matter through the Word of God. For Christians, the absolute, best way to solve any doctrinal dispute is by opening our hearts and minds in humility, and opening up our Bibles and allowing it to answer questions, clear up confusion, and quiet chaos by bringing clarity to the matter.

Of course, this also requires us to be open and to realize there may be some things about a subject we have yet to learn. If we think we *know it all* we will not be open to seeing, understanding, or learning truths that are new to us. The *know-it-all* mind-set is an obstacle to further spiritual growth because further spiritual growth begins with learning new things, or learning new things about the old things we only had a partial understanding of.

In **1 Corinthians 13:9-10** the apostle Paul wrote:

> **"<u>For we know in part</u> and we prophesy in part.**
> **¹⁰ But when that which is perfect has come,**
> **then that which is in part will be done away."**

Paul was basically saying that everything we know, regardless of how much we know, is just a part of all there is to know about a matter. It doesn't matter how much we have learned, or how long we have been saved, called, preaching, teaching, prophesying, or pastoring, *all* that we know is just a *part* of what there is to know about a subject.

When we enter discussions (or read things) being certain that our position is 100 percent right with no wiggle room for the Word of God to shed new light on subjects, we deprive ourselves of an opportunity to increase in knowledge and further spiritual development.

I have learned that when we are open to considering new things about old matters, God will give us fresh revelation that will key more revelations being unlocked to us. This is because as we value true, biblically supported revelation by not rejecting it or being opposed to considering it, we receive more revelation. We receive the reward of more revelation because we are good stewards of the revelation God shares with us, be it directly or through genuine men or women of God. If we are faithful in receiving revelation that is sown into us when it is shown to us, we will reap more and greater revelations. This applies to any biblical truths, the subject of Holy Spirit baptism and *tongues* notwithstanding.

If we are faithful in receiving revelation, we will also be receiving a key that unlocks the door to even greater treasures and hidden mysteries in the Word of God.

One of the one million reasons why I love the Bible is because it allows us to see ourselves in the life and experiences of others. In **Acts 18:24-26** we are permitted to peer into the life of a gentleman who had an unquenchable zeal for sharing the Word of God. But the Bible reveals something to us about him that allowed him to be an even greater man of God.

> **Now a certain Jew named Apollos, born at Alexandria, an eloquent man and mighty in the Scriptures, came to Ephesus. ²⁵ This man had been instructed in the way of the Lord; and being fervent in spirit, he spoke and taught accurately the things of the Lord, though he knew only the the baptism of John. ²⁶ So he began to speak boldly in the synagogue. When Aquila and Priscilla heard him, they took him aside and explained to him the way of God more accurately.**

Although Apollos was very knowledgeable of the Scriptures and had been helpful to many people in teaching what he knew, he only knew what he knew *in part*. That which he only knew *in part* had to do with baptism because **verse 25** says he "**...taught accurately the things of the Lord, though <u>he knew only the baptism of John,</u>**" which was water baptism.

In the following chapter, the apostle Paul asked a group of disciples if they "**...had received the Holy Spirit since (they) believed.**" In response, they said they had experienced "**John's** (water) **baptism.**" Paul went on to tell them that John's baptism was different from Holy Spirit baptism before laying hands on them and leading them to the baptism of the Holy Spirit.

What these twelve disciples understood about baptism was all that Apollos understood about baptism; and they both only understood *in part*. However, when Aquila and Priscilla came along, they explained to (and possibly led) Apollos to Holy Spirit baptism in the way Paul explained and led that group of disciples to being filled with the Holy Spirit.

As was the case with Apollos, it's possible for us as Christians (be we laymen, ministers, or those of the five-fold ministry) to be very knowledgeable of the Scriptures and yet only know certain things *in part*. That isn't an indictment of our knowledge, our calling, or our level of spiritual maturity. It's simply an indication that we are in very fine company with Apollos, the apostle Paul, and thousands of other men and women of God who were, and are, constantly improving and **"increasing in the knowledge of God" (Colossians 1:10)**.

Apollos would later be joined with the disciples and eventually become a very trusted and influential leader in the church after the Lord connected him with the apostle Paul. In **1 Corinthians 3:6**, Paul would later write of the partnership in the garden of God and say, **"I have planted, Apollos watered, but God gave the increase."**

Apollos' best attribute was not his eloquence or his mighty knowledge of the Scriptures. Neither was it his fervor or his sound Bible teaching. I believe his *best* attribute was his humility. It was his humility that allowed him to receive that which was *more perfect* when he only knew that which was *in part*.

It has long been my prayerful desire that the many mighty men and women of God who have only understood tongues and the other elements of Holy Spirit baptism *in part* would open their hearts in humility and receive increased understanding of this most important matter. After salvation, there is no more important occurrence in the life of the Christian than that of Holy Spirit baptism. It is important to our spiritual growth and development, it is important to our family and their future, and it is important as we go forward to serve God in whatsoever capacity we have been called and gifted in. The people we love and care for are depending on us to be as powerful as possible! Let's not let them down!

TONGUES, TONGUES, TONGUES!

PART 2 - UNDERSTANDING THE TWO TYPES OF TONGUES

Do all have gifts of healings?
Do all speak with tongues?
Do all interpret?
1 Corinthians 12:30

As I mentioned in the opening to this chapter, one of the most common beliefs is that not everyone can speak in tongues because not everyone has that *gift*.

This idea is taken from **1 Corinthians 12:30** wherein the apostle Paul asks the rhetorical question, **"Do all speak with tongues?"** Because the answer to the question is no, many have been led to believe that speaking in tongues is not one of their spiritual gifts; therefore, they cannot speak in tongues.

As odd as it may sound, to this way of thinking I would say it is both true and false that Christians cannot speak in tongues.

In order to understand this, you must first understand that there are *two different types of tongues* we're dealing with. One type, the spiritual *gift* of tongues (which is the type of tongues the apostle Paul is addressing in **1 Corinthians 12:30**), no, not everyone can speak in because, as truthfully believed by many, not everyone has that *gift*.

However, there is another type of *tongues* in the Bible that many people have not distinguished as being separate and different from the tongues referenced by Paul in **1 Corinthians 12.** That chapter begins with the words:

"Now concerning spiritual *gifts…*"

Paul then goes on to list some of the spiritual *gifts*, tongues being among them, in verse 10 and again in verse 30. *(It is also interesting and important to note that in* **1 Corinthians 12:28** *Paul wrote of* **"varieties of tongues."** *This alone allows us to know that there is more than just the* gift *of tongues that operates among believers.)*

We find this *other* type of *tongues* spoken of by Jesus in Mark's account of the Gospel.

**"And these *signs* shall follow (all) those who
believe: In My name they will cast out demons;
they will speak with new *tongues*";
Mark 16:17**

Did you catch that? Jesus speaks of *tongues* but He categorizes it as a *sign*. Paul's reference to *tongues* was under the category of a *gift*.

"And these *signs…tongues.*"
"Concerning spiritual *gifts…tongues.*"

Whereas it is true that not every Christian can speak in the tongues that is a spiritual *gift*, every Christian can in fact speak in the tongues that is a *sign*!

Before I share with you the difference in operation, purpose, and benefits, let me show you how to distinguish the *gift* of tongues in the Bible from the tongues that is a *sign*.

In **1 Corinthians 12**, every time we see the *gift* of tongues mentioned, immediately following it we find the gift of interpretation. This is because, unlike any other of the spiritual gifts, these two work together hand in hand. Take a look:

> **"...to another the working of miracles,**
> **to another prophecy, to another discerning of spirits,**
> **to another different kinds of <u>tongues</u>, to another**
> **<u>the interpretation of tongues</u>."**
> **1 Corinthians 12:10**

> **1 Corinthians 12:30**
> **"Do all have *gifts* of healings?**
> **Do all speak with <u>*tongues?*</u>**
> **Do all <u>*interpret?*</u>"**

> **1 Corinthians 14:5**
> **"...he who prophesies is greater than**
> **he who speaks with <u>*tongues*</u>, unless**
> **indeed, he <u>*interprets*</u>, that the**
> **church may receive edification."**

> **1 Corinthians 14:26**
> **"...Whenever you come together, each of you has a psalm,**
> **has a teaching, has a <u>*tongue*</u>, has a revelation, has an**
> **<u>*interpretation*</u>. Let all things be done for edification."**

In each of these passages we are allowed to know that the tongues spoken of is the spiritual *gift* because it is mentioned with the spiritual gift of interpretation. But when we find the tongues that is a *sign* (of being filled with the Holy Spirit), we do not find any references to interpretation.

Let's take a look at that, and in doing so we will see why it is held by many that tongues are a *sign*, or evidence of being Spirit filled.

We understand that the first occurrence of Holy Spirit baptism took place on the Day of Pentecost, referenced in **Acts 2:1-4**. This was not only the fulfillment of the promise of the Holy Spirit coming to help Christians; it is also the first time we find Christians speaking in tongues.

> **"And they were all <u>filled with the Holy Spirit</u>**
> **and began to <u>speak with other</u> *tongues*,**
> **as the Spirit gave the utterance."**
> **Acts 2:4**

The two points I would like you to see here are:

1) When the Holy Spirit <u>first</u> came to fill Christians, the <u>first</u> thing we see as a result of this filling is them **"speaking with other *tongues*."**

2) We can know this particular tongue was the *sign* Jesus spoke of and not the *gift* Paul spoke of because we do not find any mention of interpretation. The reason for this absence is because interpretation is a *gift* primarily purposed to work in conjunction with the *gift* of tongues, not the tongues that is a *sign* of being filled with the Holy Spirit.

Here are other examples of the tongues that is a *sign* of being baptized with the Holy Spirit not being accompanied by interpretation as we saw in Paul's writing to the church of Corinth.

> **While Peter was still speaking these words**
> (about the work, death, burial, and resurrection of Jesus) **the Holy Spirit fell upon all those who heard the word. [45] And those of the circumcision who believed were astonished, as many as came with Peter, because the gift of the Holy Spirit had been poured out on the Gentiles also.**
> **Acts 10:44-45**

What you are about to read in **verses 46-47** allows us to know how Peter and those who were with him knew that the Gentiles had received the Holy Spirit.

> **For (or, because) they <u>heard them</u>**
> **<u>speak with tongues</u> and magnify God.**
> **Then Peter answered, "Can anyone forbid water,**
> **that these should not be baptized who have**
> **received the Holy Spirit just as we have?"**

Peter and those who accompanied him <u>knew</u> these new Christians had received Holy Spirit baptism <u>because</u> they heard them speak in tongues, just as they had spoken in tongues when they were filled by the Spirit on the Day of Pentecost.

Also, we know this was not the spiritual *gift* of tongues because we don't find any mention of *interpretation.* Instead, these *tongues* were a *sign* that Jesus prophesied in **Mark 16:17**. And this *sign* served as evidence that they had been filled with the Holy Spirit.

Consider this **Acts 19:6** passage as well.

> **"And when Paul had laid hands on them,**
> **the <u>Holy Spirit came upon then, and they spoke</u>**
> **<u>with tongues</u> and prophesied."**

Again, believers in Jesus as the Messiah being filled with the Holy Spirit, and the first thing we find (as in **Acts 2** and **Acts 10**) is them speaking in tongues. Which tongues? The one that is a *sign*. How do we know this wasn't the spiritual *gift of tongues*? Simply because there is no mention of the *gift of interpretation* that partners with the gift of tongues.

For many people, including the ones in the many countries I've shared this with, this revelation of there being more than one type of *tongues* has been a tremendous blessing! This allows them to know that even though they may not be able to speak in the tongues that is a *gift*, they, and <u>every</u> Christian, can indeed speak in the tongues that is a *sign* of being filled with the Holy Spirit!

ALL MEANS ALL

Everyone who was filled in **Acts 2**, **Acts 10**, and **Acts 19** <u>all</u> spoke in tongues! And this is *exactly* what Jesus promised **Mark 16:17** when He said:

> **"And these <u>*signs*</u> shall follow (all of) those**
> **who believe...they (all) will speak**
> **with new <u>*tongues*</u>."**

> **Acts 2:4**
> **"And they were <u>all</u> filled with the**
> **Holy Spirit and (they all) began to**
> **speak with other tongues, as the**
> **Spirit gave them (all) utterance."**

> **Acts 10:44, 46**
> **"...the Holy Spirit fell upon <u>all</u> those who**
> **heard the word...they heard them**
> **(all) speak with tongues..."**

> **Acts 19:6**
> **"...the Holy Spirit came upon (all of) them,**
> **and they (all) spoke with tongues..."**

In each instance where the *tongues* that is a *sign* is mentioned, <u>*all*</u>—not just many, some, or a few—<u>*all*</u> of the people were able to speak in tongues. And they did so following the Holy Spirit filling or falling on them; indicating the tongues that is a *sign* signifies Holy Spirit baptism has taken place.

It has been my experience that once this barrier-removing revelation is received by people, they are not only open to the idea of speaking in tongues, but they are also anxious and excited about being baptized with the Holy Spirit! And when I extend an invitation for them to come, they come and they are *filled!*

> **There are two types of tongues.**
> **One every Christian <u>cannot</u> speak in,**
> **and one every Christian**
> **<u>can</u> speak in.**

I FIND NO FRUIT

People who don't embrace the biblically supported teaching of tongues being a sign of Holy Spirit baptism refute it by suggesting other things such as love, kindness, patience, etc., act as evidence of a believer having been filled. However, all of those things are *fruit* of the Spirit and do not serve as *signs* of being filled. We know this because in none of the places where we find believers being baptized in the Holy Spirit do we see any reference to love, peace, joy, kindness, or anything else. We *only* see tongues the *sign* serving as an indication the Christian had been **"endued with power."**

As with the gifts of the Spirit, the fruit of the Spirit is very important in the life of the believer. And both the gifts and the fruit are products of the working of the Holy Spirit. Whereas the gifts edify the church, the fruit of the Spirit serves more as evidence a Christian has matured or is maturing. But no mention of fruit is found in the Scriptures during the times when believers received Holy Spirit baptism. Not even one.

Although being filled with the Holy Spirit *can* help believers to bear fruit, it doesn't always do so because of the absence of cooperation from the Christian. I know Spirit-filled people who are seemingly fruitless. No love, no joy, no patience, no kindness, no goodness, no faithfulness, no gentleness, or no self-control. They have *no* fruit on their tree. Shucks, I don't even think they have any leaves! But I know Christians who are not Spirit-filled who have plenty of fruit and leaves! So being fruitful or fruitless is not always an indication of a person being filled or not being filled with the Holy Spirit.

GREAT IS THY FAIRNESS, O GOD

Aside from being a *sign* of being filled with the Holy Spirit that every Christian experiences when they are filled, I believe God also allows everyone to speak in this particular type of tongues because He wants every Christian to enjoy the benefits of doing so.

**For there is no
partiality with God.
Romans 2:11**

Because God is a fair and just God, He would not give me something to aid me in life, ministry, and my relationship with Him, and not make the same thing available to you and all of His other children. In fact, Peter makes this exact point as it applies to Holy Spirit baptism and the ability to praise and pray in tongues when he was explaining what happened when he went and ministered to Cornelius and those with him.

Then Peter opened his mouth
(Hmph, imagine that!)
**and said: "In truth I perceive
that God shows no respecter of persons."
Acts 10:34**

ONE AND ALL

The tongues that is a *sign* of being filled is purposed to benefit us *individually* as Christians, while the tongues that is a *gift* is purposed to benefit the church congregation, when properly operated along with the gift of interpretation. This is actually the case with all of the spiritual gifts. In **1 Corinthians 12**, the apostle Paul wrote:

> **"Concerning spiritual gifts...**
> **the manifestation of the Spirit is**
> **given to each one for the <u>profit of all</u>**
> *(who are in the church).*
> **1 Corinthians 12:1, 7**

The *gift* of tongues, when accompanied by the gift of interpretation, is purposed by God to build up and strengthen the entire church congregation. (This is one reason why God says in **1 Corinthians 14:39, "Do not forbid to speak in tongues."** But verse 40 goes on to say, **"Let all things be done decently and in order."**

This no doubt means that if the gift of tongues is going to operate openly in the church gathering, it should be accompanied by the gift of interpretation so the entire congregation can be edified and blessed by what God speaks to His people through the partnership of those two gifts in orderly concert.

I sincerely hope this has shed some light and cleared up any confusion or misunderstandings you may have had on the matter of tongues. I also hope any opposition or apprehension you felt towards the God-ordained spiritual element of tongues has been eliminated. And as a result, I *really* hope you're ready and willing to trust God to fill you with His Spirit and enable you to operate in the *evidence* of being *filled*.

TONGUES, TONGUES, TONGUES!

PART 3 – THE BIG, QUIET QUESTION

**I thank my God I speak with
tongues more than you all...
1 Corinthians 14:18**

As I prepare to close this chapter, I want to look at two things the apostle Paul said—one directly related to tongues and the other indirectly related to tongues.

Taken from the verse above, the first and obvious thing to recognize is that Paul, the writer of most of the New Testament, is saying not that he spoke in tongues once or twice, but that he did on a regular, ongoing basis, and he did so more than anyone in the church of Corinth. Which means that at the very time he was writing this letter that would later become a part of the Holy Scriptures God would use to lead millions to salvation and maturity in Jesus Christ, Paul was speaking in tongues. I had never considered that before this exact moment as I'm writing this, but this blows my mind to consider!

And as cool as that is to consider, what's cooler, more telling, and more compelling than that is the fact that Paul opens up that verse by saying, **"*I thank my God* I speak with tongues more than you all."**

There must have been something pretty special about speaking in tongues that caused Paul to *thank God* for the ability to do so. And what's interesting about Paul *thanking God* for being able to speak in tongues is the fact that many who highly respect Paul don't want to have anything to do with the tongues he found value in enough to *thank God* for. That's perplexing.

Follow the Leader

The other thing I would like to point out is that Paul, during the writing of this letter (and during the time he was speaking in tongues more than everyone in the Corinthian church), said in **1 Corinthians 11:1, "Imitate me, just as I also imitate Christ."**

In place of the term, *imitate me*, other translations use terms such as: *"Be followers of me; take me for your example; copy my example;* and *pattern yourselves after me." And* one of my favorites, from the KSBMIPT, *"Do what I did!"*

The apostle Paul, whom we hold in high esteem, proudly spoke in tongues. And his living, Holy Spirit inspired words to us are, **"Imitate me, just as I also imitate Christ."**

Now, there may be a tendency to think Paul is only talking about *imitating* him as it pertains to the things chapter 10 concludes with. But I think it's safe to say that the scope of his advice includes *everything* that was good and godly about him. Certainly, speaking in tongues was good because he thanked God for the ability to do so. And of course, speaking in tongues was godly because the ability to do so was enabled by God's Spirit.

**I thank God
I speak with tongues.**

Imitating Christ

Paul may have primarily been talking about imitating Christ in character, but imitating Christ also in the things He did would also be a great idea. Paul spoke in tongues, so is that one of the things he was **"imitating Christ"** in doing? That's a good question because some have asked, *"If tongues are so important, why didn't Jesus speak in tongues?"* This is the big, quiet question! This is what I call *an* *assertive question* because it is not asking whether or not Jesus spoke in tongues. Instead, it is questioning the importance of speaking in tongues by asserting that Jesus did *not* speak in tongues.

This assertive question was one of the many I had in mind when asking the Lord to help me to answer all of the questions concerning Holy Spirit baptism. It was also a question many who speak in tongues have curiously and quietly wondered about. After all, tongues are a *sign* of being filled with the Holy Spirit and Jesus was filled with the Holy Spirit, so why *didn't* He speak in tongues like everyone else we see in the Bible who had been filled with the Holy Spirit?

When we have questions with no answers, another thing that happens is that we tend to allow the assertions or suggestions of others to serve as our answers. When people imply that Jesus didn't speak in tongues, because I had a question with no answer, I subscribed to the notion that Jesus had never spoken in tongues.

That is, until the day I was reading my Bible and came across a story in **Mark 5** for maybe the fiftieth time in all of my years of reading, studying, and teaching the Bible. Mark records the story of Jairus, **"one of the rulers of the synagogue,"** whose daughter had become extremely ill. In fact, in the words of Jairus, **"My little daughter lies at the point of death."** After a brief, Spirit-orchestrated interruption from a woman got the attention of Jesus by touching the hem of His garment, Jesus and His disciples followed the heartsick but faith-filled father to his home, even after receiving word that his daughter had died. On their way, Jesus said to him, **"Do not be afraid; only believe."**

Upon their arrival, and after some human housecleaning of people whose lack of faith did not help create an environment conducive to miracles, Jesus, Peter, James, and John entered the room where the damsel lay. Here is what took place next:

**Then Jesus took the child by the hand,
and said to her, "Talitha, cumi," which is
translated, "Little girl, I say to you, arise."
Immediately the girl arose and walked,
for she was twelve years of age. And they
were overcome with great amazement.
Mark 5:41-42**

When I sat to read my Bible that day it was simply a part of my daily devotional time. I wasn't studying for a message or anything else. But when I saw the term, **"Talitha, cumi,"** I knew in that moment the question of *"Why didn't Jesus speak in tongues?"* had been answered! The answer was, He did! Jesus did speak in tongues, but I, and thousands of others who have read this (and other verses we will see in a moment) had simply overlooked it! One reason I believe I had overlooked it is because, before this moment, when I considered my use of tongues, and that of others, it had always been long and lengthy expressions. Never anything brief like, **"Talitha, cumi."**

I knew in that instance the Spirit of God was showing me Jesus speaking in tongues! Personally, I was satisfied with that revelation because I had come to learn how it feels when the Holy Spirit was unlocking unto me one of the mysteries and hidden truths of the Word of God; but, I needed more if I was going to make a case for it in teaching others. Revelation without biblical confirmation is merely speculation. And the absent evidence may cause the carrier of revelation to be considered crazy or incredible, at best. The rest of that day I was consumed with confirming the fact that Jesus had indeed spoken in tongues.

As is typical for me when I encounter spiritual things that I consider *uncommon*, I spent hours in that day, and in subsequent days, looking for evidence that would convince a jury of Christians of my new findings. It's not enough for the trial attorney to know the truth. They must be able to provide support for that truth that will persuade a judge or a jury.

In looking again at **Mark 5:41**, after the phrase **"Talitha cumi,"** what got my attention was the word, **"translated."** The only time words are translated is when they are foreign to the hearers or the readers. **"Talitha cumi"** was not the language used by the people Jesus was ministering to or Jesus Himself. For if it had been it would have been translated into English, simply to read, **"Little girl, I say to you, arise"** with the exclusion of **"Talitha cumi"** in the text. But the very fact that a non-English term was allowed to remain in its original offering says that it very well may have been unknown to Jesus and the others.

Some have suggested that **"Talitha cumi"** was not tongues but it was the Aramaic language Jesus and His disciples (and the people they ministered to) were all learned in. For support they point to similar Aramaic words being feminine in nature like *talitha,* and Aramaic words similar to *cumi* that mean, "to stand." But the question would then be, if Jesus spoke Aramaic (though He may have spoken other languages as well) and *talitha cumi* is Aramaic, why wouldn't *talitha cumi* have been translated along with every-thing else Jesus spoke in that verse, chapter, and book, and simply rendered, **"Little girl, I say to you arise"**? Why would the trans-lators from Aramaic (or any other language Jesus may have spoken in) leave that term in its original language but translate everything else Jesus said? Before one can discredit **"Talitha cumi"** being tongues, they would have to make sense of these questions.

Mark was not present to translate this for the hearers at the time, but after having been told of the situation by Peter, James, and/or John, Mark was later inspired, perhaps through the gift of interpretation, to know the meaning, and under the inspira-tion of the Holy Spirit, to include it in his Gospel account. In this consideration it is also interesting that neither Matthew nor Luke's account of this story includes the phrase, **"Talitha cumi,"** and it probably is because they were not familiar with the term (if it were Aramaic and they spoke Aramaic they most certainly would be familiar with it) and could not interpret what it meant.

Therefore, they were not allowed by the Spirit to address it in their documentation of the Gospel.

> Tongues is a
> legitimate language
> from somewhere in
> the world.

During the time of my study and research on Jesus speaking in tongues in **Mark 5**, I was led to two other instances in the book of Mark that demonstrate further support for this finding. Here's the next one:

Mark 7:32-35
**Then they brought to Jesus one who was
deaf and had an impediment in his speech,
and they begged Him to put His hand on him.
[33] And Jesus took him aside from the
multitude, and put His fingers in his ears,
and He spat and touched his tongue.
[34] Then, looking up to heaven, He sighed,
and said to him, "Ephphatha," that is,
"Be opened." [35] Immediately his ears were
opened, and the impediment of his tongue
was loosed, and he spoke plainly.**

Here again we find what I believe is another example of Jesus speaking in tongues that I had also overlooked because it did not fit the mode of my experience with tongues being long, flowing, and ongoing instead of very brief expressions.

The story of this particular miracle of Jesus is only found in Mark's gospel. And again, Mark was able to translate the tongue and reveal the meaning to the reader. But the same questions exist in this scenario. If this was *the language of the day*, why wasn't the word **"Ephphatha"** converted and dropped like the other words of that language? I think the answer is because it wasn't an expression of the language Jesus commonly spoke. I believe it was allowed to remain through the translation process so people would come to realize that Jesus, being filled with the Holy Spirit, spoke in tongues just as every other Spirit-filled person can do.

> **We have been thrown off by the brevity of the tongues spoken in by Jesus.**

The final Bible record of Jesus speaking in tongues is in the story we are most familiar with, as it is one of the most captivating occurrences in the life of Jesus and in the history of mankind. This account took place in a city outside of Jerusalem, at a place called Calvary, on a cross where He died for you and me.

> **Now when the sixth hour had come, there was darkness over the whole land until the ninth hour. And at the ninth hour Jesus cried out with a loud voice, saying, "Eloi, Eloi, lama sabachthani?" which is translated, "My God, My God, why have You forsaken Me?"**
> **Mark 15:33-34**

According to Mark and Matthew, the very last words spoken by our Savior from the cross was an expression in tongues. As long as I have believed and taught that this was tongues, not until this moment had I considered that these were at least among the last words uttered by Jesus before He died for our sins. That's interesting, to say the least. Why didn't Jesus just say, *"My God, My God, why have You forsaken Me?"* in His own language? We have given Jesus credit for saying what Mark translated in his writing, but in His own language, Jesus didn't actually say, *"My God, My God, why have You forsaken Me?"* Instead, what He literally said was, **"Eloi, Eloi, lama sabachthani?"**

But why didn't Jesus just say that in a language that all who were present could have understood? Maybe it was because of His mother, brothers, sister, disciples, and other followers. Maybe Jesus didn't want them to hear the words that suggested, He Whom they had been following and trusting for salvation was wavering, believing that His God and Father had forsaken Him. Maybe the Spirit expressed what was on the mind of Jesus through tongues out of concern for what it may have done to the faith of the followers of Jesus.

As leaders, the one thing we want to guard against is the appearance of wavering in our faith in God in the presence of those we lead. Sure, we wonder and waver, but we should do so outside of their presence because what may be a temporary lapse of faith for us could become a long-term lapse of faith for them. So perhaps Jesus spoke in a language none of them understood in an effort to safeguard their faith in the Father during the traumatic death of His Son.

WHY SO SHORT?

Some may wonder, *"Why doesn't the Bible reveal Jesus speaking in tongues for longer periods of time?"* That's a great question! I would imagine that Jesus did spend a significant amount of time praying in the Spirit when no one else was around. Remember, there were times when He was praying overnight when everyone else was asleep, and other times when He went and prayed alone in different places. Even if His disciples or others had been near to hear Jesus praying in the Spirit, they would not have understood what He was saying. No one would have been able to understand what Jesus was praying because no one was able to interpret tongues. This was because the Holy Spirit had not yet come and given that ability to anyone. Another possible reason as to why the disciples seemingly did not hear Jesus speak in tongues during His prayer time was because they may have been alarmed by what they heard, just as people today are alarmed by hearing what they haven't been taught and don't understand.

It really shouldn't be a surprise that Jesus spoke in tongues. Why wouldn't He? He had been baptized in the Holy Spirit. Why wouldn't His life manifest the evidence of having been filled? And, since He experienced trials and temptations as we do, why wouldn't He have used tongues to help Himself just as tongues can be used to help us? It just stands to reason that Jesus would have spoken in tongues.

And when it comes to *us* utilizing the tongues that is a *sign* of having been baptized in the Holy Spirit, doing so on a regular basis benefits and blesses us, greatly!

In chapter 6 you will see just how *great* some of those benefits are. But first, check out chapter 5! It's fascinating!

CHAPTER 5

FASCINATING PERSONAL AND
SCIENTIFIC FINDINGS

**For if I pray in a tongue,
my spirit prays, but my
understanding is unfruitful
1 Corinthians 14:14**

Aside from it being the miraculous first manifestation of Holy Spirit baptism, there are a number of other amazing aspects concerning this spiritual phenomenon. One such thing is that the practice of tongues serves as evidence that it is not us praising or praying in the Spirit, but it truly is the Spirit Himself offering intercessory praise and prayer to the Father on our behalf.

The fascinating fact about this is, when the Holy Spirit prays and gives praise for us, it leaves our mind free to do other things that we would otherwise need it to be focusing on. For example, one morning, years ago, I was in my prayer room where I also do my praise and worship, Bible reading, and write whatever the Lord may choose to share with me during that time. Sometimes it's nothing; sometimes it's very much! On this particular morning, after singing and dancing before the Lord *(Hey! If it was good enough for David, the worshiping warrior, it's good enough for me!)*, the Lord began to share some things with me while I praising and praying in tongues. When I realized that it was more than just a thought, I grabbed a pen and tablet and begin to write what He was sharing.

I don't recall whether it was words for a teaching I was to do sometime soon, or just something He was sharing for the sake of me knowing, or perhaps, teaching sometime later. What I do remember is, after I began writing and had been writing for a few minutes, I had not stopped speaking in tongues. As I was speaking in the Spirit I was still able to fluently write the things God was giving me.

This may not sound like a big deal until you consider the fact that it is naturally impossible for us to talk and write at the same time. The reason for this is because we need our mind to communicate to our mouth what to say, or we need our mind to instruct our hand on what is to be written. Our mind is not capable of simultaneously feeding our mouth what to say and our hand what to write. It has to do either one or the other. Therefore, we can only do one or the other. If we speak, we cannot write. If we write, we cannot speak. Only one at a time, writing or speaking, can draw from the well of our mind. *(Try it and you'll see how interrupted and unfocused your speaking or writing will be!)*

But when I was speaking in tongues with my mouth, my hand was still writing the things the Lord was sharing with me. The *only* way this could have been possible is for that which was coming out of my mouth to not have been a product of _my_ mind, but a work of the Holy Spirit! I know this because I was using my mind to communicate to my hand what to write, while the Holy Spirit was communicating with my mouth what to speak. That's fascinating!

In fact, it was while I was praising in the Spirit in my office that it came to mind to add this part to the book. And literally, while I was writing this with my hand, I was speaking in the Spirit with my mouth!

WE CAN'T TALK AND READ AT THE SAME TIME...CAN WE?

Sometime after learning this was possible, I somehow came up with the idea of attempting to read the Bible while speaking in tongues. The same thing applies as it pertains to the mind. When we are reading our mind is occupied with comprehending what we are reading. Therefore, we are typically not capable of reading and talking at the same time. But I decided to try to speak in tongues and *read* at the same time. So I tried it. And...I did it! I was able to speak in tongues and read with complete comprehension! And I was amazed! I was astonished! I was astounded, bewildered, blown away, dazed, dumbfounded, ecstatic, impressed, shocked, staggered, and stunned! But you can probably tell that I wasn't excited, though.

**We can praise, pray, and read or write
at the same time.
Yes! Multitasking in the Spirit!**

THE FASCINATING SCIENTIFIC FINDING ABOUT TONGUES

Some years ago, I viewed a video clip from the *ABC News* program, *Nightline Online.* The program featured a doctor, who by all accounts was not a Christian *(or at the very least not a Christian who practiced speaking in tongues or who was looking to support the practice)* but was simply *"looking for an explanation for what many regard as (inexplicable)"* according to the story's reporter. The doctor engaged two people who spoke in tongues to volunteer for the study: one male, one female. One a pastor; the other may or may not have been a member of the Christian clergy. Separately, the doctor performed two sets of scans on their brain. The first while they were praying in English (their natural language), and the second while they prayed in tongues (the foreign, unlearned language).

The apparatus used was designed to detect brain activity during the time when they prayed in English and when they prayed in tongues. What was revealed in the results of the two persons, with the two separate testings, was the same result. When they prayed in English (meaning they were choosing the words to say to God in prayer) the *frontal lobe,* the part of the brain that is normally activated by language, was "active." However, when the same test was conducted and the participants spoke in tongues, the frontal lobe "fell quiet," indicating it did not sense any activity of language being used.

How is that possible? It is possible because when we pray or praise in tongues, it is *not us* using our efforts or language to do so; it is the Holy Spirit. When *we* praise or pray in our learned language(s), we are thinking of what to say and that is the activity that takes place in the frontal lobe of our brain. But when the Spirit of God praises or prays on our behalf in tongues, there is no frontal lobe activity. There is no brain activity because it is not *us* using our brain to think of words to say to God; it is the Holy Spirit making intercessory offerings of praise and prayer for us to our heavenly Father! This is how I was able to read and write while praising and praying in the Spirit.

This is not only fascinating but it also serves as scientific evidence that tongues is not just a series of words and sounds that Christians make up, but it is, in fact, a true, supernatural work of God. And through the baptism of the Holy Spirit, tongues is available to Christian men and woman, from the pulpit to the pew, in Africa, the Americas, Asia, Australia, Antarctica, and Europe! For God is not a respecter of persons. Jesus will baptize every Christian, everywhere, enabling us all to pray and praise the Father, in the Spirit!

CHAPTER 6

THE HELP,
THE BLESSINGS, AND THE BENEFITS

**"...I will pray the Father,
and He will give you another Helper..."
John 14:16**

The role of the Holy Spirit as a helper in our life begins with our acceptance of Jesus as Savior sent by the Father. At that point, the Holy Spirit spiritually baptizes us into the body of believers, making us a part of the Christian family with all of the entitlements that accompany that prestigious honor.

There are many other ways the Holy Spirits helps us. These include but are not limited to: teaching us, leading and guiding us, convicting our conscience, spiritual fruit, spiritual gifts, talents, and abilities, and the anointing that enables us to effectively function in serving God. There are other ways the Holy Spirit helps us that are not mentioned here, and some I have yet to learn.

The Holy Spirit enabling us to speak in tongues helps us through a completely separate set of blessings and benefits.

To see some of these blessings and benefits, let's go back to when the Holy Spirit first filled believers and they first spoke in tongues as a *sign* of being filled.

> **Acts 2:4-11**
> **And they were all filled with the Holy Spirit**
> **and began to speak with other tongues, as the**
> **Spirit gave them utterance. ⁵ And there were**
> **dwelling in Jerusalem Jews, devout men, from**
> **every nation under heaven. ⁶ And when this**
> **sound occurred, the multitude came together,**
> **and were confused, because <u>everyone heard them</u>**
> **<u>speak in his own language</u>. ⁷ Then they were**
> **all amazed and marveled, saying to one another,**
> **"Look, are not all these who speak Galileans?**
> **⁸ And <u>how is it that we hear, each in our own</u>**
> **<u>language in which we were born</u>? ⁹ Parthians**
> **and Medes and Elamites, those dwelling in**
> **Mesopotamia, Judea and Cappadocia, Pontus**
> **and Asia, ¹⁰ Phrygia and Pamphylia, Egypt and**
> **the parts of Libya adjoining Cyrene, visitors**
> **from Rome, both Jews and proselytes,**
> **¹¹ Cretans, and Arabs—we hear them speaking**
> **in our own tongues the wonderful works of God."**

It's important to understand that tongues is not just a bunch of jibber-jabber or made-up sounds, syllables, and sayings. Tongues are a legitimate language from somewhere in the world of which the believer who is baptized with the Holy Spirit is able to speak by Him.

We know and have heard about the miracle-working power of the Holy Spirit in healing sicknesses, cleansing from diseases, delivering from demons, restoring sight and hearing and the ability to talk and walk, and the casting out of devils and the raising of the dead. But before any of those miracles happened, the miraculous ability to speak in a language the disciples had not studied and learned was the first to take place!

Anyone who is filled with the Holy Spirit, evidenced by the *sign* of tongues, has, by those tongues, been supernaturally

enabled to speak in a legitimate foreign language and has personally experienced the miracle-working power of the Holy Spirit!
That's exciting!!

**Tongues is not just a bunch of
jibber-jabber; it is a legitimate
language from somewhere in the world.**

The next thing we see in that passage concerning their new,
legitimate foreign language, is what someone identified them as
saying when they were speaking in tongues, **"...we hear them
speaking in <u>our own language</u> *the wonderful works of God.*"**

Anytime anyone speaks *"the wonderful works of God"* they
are *praising* God. The very first time the very first disciples spoke in
tongues, it was the very first *praise offering* of the New Testament
church.

David, who was not only the king of Israel, but I believe to also
have been the king of praise, declared in **Psalm 26:7, "That I may
proclaim with the voice of thanksgiving, and tell of all Your
wondrous works."

The king of praise would also say to the King of Glory, **"Many,
O LORD my GOD, are Your *wonderful works* which You have
done; And Your thoughts towards us cannot be recounted to
You in order; If I would declare and speak of them, they are
more than can be numbered."**

The point is, when the "wonderful works" of God are spoken
of, the God of the "wonderful works" is being praised. And this was
the case with the first time tongues was spoken by the believers in
Acts 2.

Praise is important for a number of reasons. In my book, *Trouble:
What Every Christian Should Know About Trials, Tribulations, and
Troublesome Times,* I dedicated an entire chapter to the importance

of praise and how many people in the Bible used praise strategically during their days of difficulty.

And if our praise from the words of our own understanding is helpful, how much more is the Spirit-inspired miraculous praise of tongues? That's both a benefit and a blessing of being filled with the Holy Spirit, being able to *praise God in the Spirit*!

NEXT!

After giving our life to Christ by repenting from our sin and believing in Him as the Savior, the next most important thing is to be filled with the Holy Spirit. Holy Spirit baptism is important because it is essential to our spiritual growth.

Many Christians who are sincere in their belief in Jesus as the Savior struggle mightily with sin, bad habits, and bad attitudes because they don't grow. In fact, many people fall away from God because they don't experience the spiritual growth that helps to root and ground us in our relationship with Him. The ability to speak in tongues provides many benefits and blessings, including help in overcoming sin and growing spiritually.

MY PERSONAL FILLING WITH NO FEELING

The following verse is the verse that single-handedly led me to being filled with the Holy Spirit about six months after I gave my life to Christ. One morning in the winter of 1989, I was minding my own business and reading my Bible, when I came across **1 Corinthians 14:4.** The verse read, **"He who speaks in a tongue edifies himself."** Although the verse didn't speak directly about being filled with the Spirit, it offered something I wanted—to be *edified,* built up, and strengthened in Christ.

In order to get to this place of being stronger in the Lord, I had to take the path of *speaking in tongues*. I didn't know anything about tongues. I hadn't heard teachings; neither had I read any material on the matter. I didn't think about it in that moment, but

I later recalled hearing my mother speak in tongues in the days of my heathenism. And it may have been a good thing that I didn't think about it then, because back in those days, I really thought, *"Mom, you've gone too far!"* So I may not have been interested.

(Notice, I said, "I...thought." I would not have dared to <u>say</u> such a thing. Even though my mother was extremely loving, kind, sweet, saved, and filled with the Holy Spirit, she wasn't putting up with any of my nonsense. All she had to do was say, "Boy, you betta...!" Sometimes all she had to do was give me <u>that look</u> and I knew what that meant and what may have followed if I didn't exit stage left! In Trouble *I wrote about the time she made me think I was an astronaut by causing me to see stars!)*

The talk in **1 Corinthians 14:4** of speaking in tongues and being be built up in the Lord didn't bother me one bit! I was so thirsty for God and so trusting of His Word that whatever He said or however He led, I was willing to follow!

I didn't read further than that verse before I simply said to the Lord, *"Father, I don't know what this speaking in tongues thing is all about, but if it will help me to be built up in You, okay, I want it."* The next morning while I was in prayer, it happened! I began speaking in tongues! No one was there to lay hands on me or to walk me through the process I typically walk people through when I teach and minister Holy Spirit baptism. It just happened!

I didn't feel warm or fuzzy. I didn't fall out or faint. I didn't feel an electric current, do the electric-slide, or hear angels singing, though there may have been a couple of dogs barking in the background. I didn't see, sense, hear, smell, or feel anything. I just spoke in tongues. That was all I needed because that is the only sign we find when the Holy Spirit first filled the apostles on the Day of Pentecost and during subsequent fillings in the Bible.

It was odd in that it was new to me, but it was odd also because while I was speaking in tongues with my mouth, I was analyzing the sound with my mind. I remember thinking that it sounded like a language from East Asia. Possibly Japanese or Chinese. I wondered if my final Army duty assignment in Okinawa, Japan had anything to do with that. Whatever the case, I was ecstatic that God had heard me, and that my Lord had answered my request!

I wasn't going to allow <u>not</u> speaking in tongues to keep me from growing in God.

One of the things I learned early on about my newfound ability to speak in tongues was that I could start and stop when I chose to. There are instances when, during our times of praise or prayer, that the Holy Spirit will begin to praise or pray in tongues on our behalf, without our prompting. But, He will never do so in a time or place where it is inappropriate or potentially embarrassing for us. Neither will the Holy Spirit initiate tongues when it is not decent or orderly to do so. In my experience it has typically been when I am in my private time of devotion. If I praise or pray in the Spirit in public, it's *silent, to myself* (**1 Corinthians 14:28**), and unnoticeable to others.

I love that we can begin and end speaking in tongues whenever we choose because it's simply another tool or **"weapon of our warfare"** we can use during our walk with God—a walk that sometimes takes us through faith fights and battlefields!

> **For though we walk in the flesh,**
> **we do not war according to the flesh.**
> **For the weapons of our warfare are**
> **not carnal but mighty in God**
> **for pulling down strongholds.**
> **2 Corinthians 10:3-4**

Another benefit of speaking in tongues is, it builds us up *in* and *on* the saving faith we have placed in Jesus. Jude, the half-brother of Jesus, confirmed this of speaking in tongues though he referred to it as "**...praying in the Holy Spirit...**"

> **"But you, beloved,**
> <u>**building up yourselves**</u>
> **on your most holy faith,**
> <u>**praying in the Holy Spirit...**</u>"
> **Jude 1:20**

From **Acts 2** we saw how tongues was first used in <u>*praising in the Spirit*</u>. Here we see tongues being encouraged for <u>*praying in the Spirit*</u>. Praying in the Holy Spirit helps to build us up in a number of ways. Let me show you just a few of the ways the Holy Spirit has taught me that tongues helps to build us up.

> **Romans 8:26**
> **Likewise, the Spirit also <u>helps</u> in our**
> **weaknesses. For we do not know what we**
> **should pray for as we ought, but <u>the Spirit</u>**
> <u>**Himself makes intercession for us**</u> **with**
> **groanings which cannot be uttered.**

This is an extremely powerful verse packed with the depth of how the Holy Spirit, through us speaking in tongues, helps to build us up.

The first thing I'd like to point out is support of the fact that **"praying in the Holy Spirit"** is the same as *the Spirit making intercession*. This is simply because to *make intercession* means to pray on someone's behalf. We pray or intercede for others because we have somehow come to know that they stand in need of something God is able to provide or perform.

Identically, when we pray in the Holy Spirit through tongues, He is making intercession for us to the Father because He knows the Father has the power to provide *for us,* or to produce *in us* that in which He is praying for on our behalf. Verse 26 gives us a general but powerful idea of the things the Holy Spirit is praying for us about when we pray in tongues, or are praying in the Spirit.

The first thing verse 26 says is, **"...the Spirit helps in our** <u>**weaknesses**</u>**..."** The idea of being *helped with our weaknesses* by nature means to be made stronger. Getting stronger automatically and simultaneously means becoming less weak. So in helping us to overcome our weakness by allowing the Holy Spirit to intercede for us through tongues, we are also being strengthened, edified, and *built up on our most holy faith.*

The original Greek word for "weaknesses" can be applied to a frailty in the mind or in the body. As it pertains to the *body* a weakness could mean some sort of physical ailment—a sickness or disease perhaps. So it is plausible, if not flat-out factual, that when we pray in the Spirit through tongues, one area of *weakness* we are helped with is in our body. There are a number of ways we can be helped with our physical infirmities when we allow the Holy Spirit to intercede for us in tongues:

1) It could lead us to the knowledge of the fact that something is wrong so we can get it checked out and treated.
2) It could lead us to know where to go or how to treat the condition.
3) It could lead to the Father performing another miracle for us and supernaturally healing the infirmity in our body.

My position on healing has long been, however it comes, thank You, Lord!

The point is, according to the Spirit-inspired writing of the apostle Paul, allowing the Holy Spirit to pray for us when we pray in tongues can help with our health.

> **Being strengthened by allowing the Holy Spirit to intercede for us through tongues weakens our weaknesses.**

Not only does the Spirit's intercession for us help with the weaknesses of our body, but our mind, as well. This is particularly helpful when it comes to the moral aspect of our being. The moral or immoral choices we make are thoughts of our mind that have graduated into our actions.

Of course this is good when we're making good, wholesome, loving, kind, and moral choices. It's not so good, however, when we're making harmful, hateful, unkind, uncaring, and immoral choices. These latter choices are products of a mind that needs to be strengthened and thereby able to control the weak, natural-minded man and not do the thing he tries to influence us to do.

Not only is our natural man producing thoughts that are designed to become immoral actions, but the devil, through *"fiery darts,"* is also making deposits into our mind in hopes of leading us to sabotaging our relationship with God and others, while lessening the quality of our natural and spiritual life. Even jeopardizing our salvation. *(Yes, that is very possible! The Bible provides dozens of verses in support of this reality!)* But even when it comes to our moral frailties, *"the Spirit also helps in our weaknesses"* by interceding for us to the Father when we pray in tongues.

> **Praying in tongues aids us in our aim for moral maturity.**

GET THE SPOON, SON

Also, when it comes to the emotional aspect of our being, which is also born in our mind and carried out in our actions, expressions, and our behavior, praying in the Spirit will help us to overcome anger, envy, jealousy, insecurity, extreme emotionalism, sadness, sorrow, depression, suicidal tendencies, passive-aggressiveness, or even fearfulness.

In **2 Timothy 1** the apostle Paul wrote to one of his sons in the faith who was pastoring the church in Ephesus. In **verse 6** he said to Timothy, **"Therefore I remind you to *stir up the gift* of God which is *in* you through the laying on of my hands."**

There are a number of very interesting things that will be very helpful for us to understand about the apostle Paul's words to Timothy. The first is that in telling Timothy to **"stir up the gift"** he is encouraging him to get back to praising and praying in the Spirit, which he was able to do because of the **"gift"** of the Holy Spirit that *filled* him.

Also, in saying **"stir up the gift"** Paul was reminding Timothy and making the point to us that we start speaking in tongues whenever we choose. There isn't a more important time to pray in the Spirit than the time we are facing adversity of some sort.

Another thing to understand is that Paul is speaking to a pastor and offering him encouragement and instruction on how to overcome something that is plaguing him emotionally. We know Timothy was being greatly affected by something or some *things* (possibly having to do with the weight of the ministry) because in verse 4 Paul said he was **"...mindful of (his) tears..."**

I realize there are some pastors who have never experienced anything that has brought them to tears, but believe me, they are the exceptions, not the rule. Most pastors who have a genuine heart for people and ministry have shed tears, either in sharing the pain of people, ministry circumstances, their private lives, or all three. I certainly have—and on more than one occasion. It comes with the calling and it's a sign of passion, compassion, and humanness. Even Jesus wept!

It was Paul's mindfulness of Timothy's emotional struggle, a struggle that not only brought him to tears, but one that also attacked his faith in God, that caused Paul to encourage him to put to use his Spirit-given ability to pray in tongues.

In verse 5, as any good father in the ministry does when they see a son or daughter struggling, Paul reaffirmed his belief in Timothy by saying, **"...I call to remembrance the genuine faith that is in you..."** And as if that wasn't enough, or to further reassure Timothy of his confidence in him, Paul reiterates his feelings just a few words later, **"...I am persuaded (that genuine faith) is in you..."**

And in verse 7, Paul reminded Timothy that **"...God has not given us a spirit of fear, but of power and of love and of a sound mind."** The fact that Paul had to remind him of this says that Timothy had allowed **"the spirit of fear"** to steal his faith and caused him the grief that brought him to tears.

But sandwiched between the *presence of tears* in verse 4 and the **"spirit of fear"** *in* verse 7 is the solution for them both, in verse 6.

> **"...stir up the gift of God (the Holy Spirit) which is in you through the laying on of my hands."**

When Paul *reminds* Timothy to **"stir up the gift"** of the Holy Spirit, he is encouraging him to get back to praying in the Spirit, knowing how much doing so would benefit him at such a time in his life.

> **Stirring up the gift of the Holy Spirit by praying in tongues helps us to get back the faith the enemy has stolen through fear!**

HE KNOWS WHAT WE KNOW NOT

The Bible does not tell us specifically what it was that was troubling Timothy. Paul may not have been intimately acquainted with the situation considering the fact that he was imprisoned and not in close proximity or communication with Timothy. And it is very possible Timothy may not have understood what was going on or why things were going wrong. We have times like that in life. No Christian of any level of maturity is completely exempt from such situations. Inexplicable trouble sometimes comes uninvited, and we may not know what to do or how to pray about it.

But consider also from **Romans 8:26** that Paul writes about the Holy Spirit's intercession for us, that **"…we do not know what we should pray for as we ought."**

It is both helpful and reassuring to know that when we pray in tongues the Holy Spirit is not only praying for us concerning our weaknesses, but He is also praying for things concerning our weaknesses that we: 1) do not know *what* to pray about them, 2) do not know *how* to pray for them.

There are times in our life, whether with us personally, our loved ones, or someone else we've prayed for, that after having prayed about a situation so long, we no longer know what else to pray or *how* else to pray about certain situations.

This is one reason why **Ephesians 6:18** says we should be **"…praying always with <u>all</u> prayer and supplication <u>in the Spirit</u>…"**

When we pray in the Holy Spirit, He knows *exactly* what and how to pray for us, our loved ones, or whomever we're praying for. The Holy Spirit knows because the Holy Spirit shares in the omniscience (all-knowing ability) of God the Father. He knows absolutely everything about every area of everyone's life. There isn't anything the Holy Spirit doesn't know. He knows everything all at once and He has never had to learn any of it! He just *knows* and He has *always known!*

He knows everything about the past, the present, the future, and all of the parties, powers, and principalities that are visibly and invisibly involved. He knows it all and He takes it all into account when He prays for us and others. He is the only true and living *Mr. Know-it-all!* Therefore, when He makes intercession through our use of tongues, He takes everything into consideration that He knows about the situation.

> **It is impossible for God to learn because He knows everything about everything, and everyone. And He has known what our days would hold, even before our days were here.**

Another powerful and important factor in the **Romans 8** passage is **verse 27**, which says the Holy Spirit **"makes intercession for the saints according to the will of God."** This is powerful and important for at least two reasons. First, the Spirit's intercession for us is automatically according to the will of God because He and the Father share the same mind. So as He is praying for us, He can *only* pray God's will. There are no prayers that are more perfectly aligned with the will of God than prayers offered by the Spirit of God, through tongues.

This leads us to the second reason why this is imperative and meaningful. **First John 5:14-15** says:

> **Now this is the confidence that we have in (God), that if we ask anything according to <u>His will</u>, He hears us. [15] And if we know that He hears us, whatever we ask, we know that we have the petitions that we have asked of Him.**

When the Holy Spirit, through tongues, **"makes intercession for (us) according to the will of God,"** God says that He hears that intercession. And *because* that intercession on our behalf is in perfect accordance with God's will, He has promised to provide the petitions that have been offered for us by His Spirit. That's powerful, and very encouraging! That's powerful and encouraging because we don't always know what the will of God is for every situation. But the Holy Spirit does! And that's *exactly* what He prays for us about, through tongues!

Limited Knowledge, Limited Prayers*

When we pray with our learned languages, we are praying **"with the understanding"** of what we're saying when we pray **(1 Corinthians 14:5)**. But those prayers, though they be sincere and fervent, are limited to the knowledge we have about the situation we're praying about *because* we are not omniscient like the Holy Spirit.

Consider this example. If someone asks us to pray for them and writes down ten prayer requests on a two-sided blackboard, five on each side, but they only show us one side of the blackboard, we can only pray for the five things we can see because we have no idea of what's on the other side of the blackboard. But the Holy Spirit does. And through our praying in the Spirit He intercedes for the things that are on the other side of the blackboard, that *we cannot see!*

We don't know everything that is happening with our spouse in their absence or in their silence. Neither do we know what is going on with our children when they are away from us. We don't know what is happening with our business or place of employment in the next two years. Nor do we know the desires of the devil in the next two weeks. But the Holy Spirit does. And He prays for us concerning those things that we *do not* know!

Whether it's our life, the life of a loved one, or the life of others we find ourselves praying for, there is *always* the *other side of the blackboard* that contains things that are invisible to our mind; things we therefore don't know *to* pray for, or *how* to pray for **"as we ought."**

But because **"all things are naked and open to the eyes of"** the Holy Spirit, He sees in places that are hidden, or dark to us. He sees things in the darkness as if the darkness is the light. Hidden things are exposed to Him as if they are common knowledge to kids.

ANOTHER PRAYER PARTNER

Praise God for our prayer partners and the prayer group we are a part of. But there is not a more powerful prayer partner to have than the Holy Spirit! Let's allow Him to make intercession for us and through us, when we pray in the Spirit!

Something that is comforting to know about the Holy Spirit interceding according to the will of God is, **Romans 12:2** teaches us that God's will is, **"...good, acceptable, and perfect."**

The words **"good, acceptable, and perfect"** in the original Greek provisions also mean *beneficial; fulfilling and well pleasing; integrity, growth, and maturity.*

When we trust God and embrace the tongues the disciples praised in on the Day of Pentecost and that Paul and every other apostle and New Testament writer spoke in, we too will begin to experience all of the help, blessings, and benefits of doing so.

As we close this chapter, I ask you again…when you consider the *tremendous help, blessings, and* benefits that are unlocked by praising and praying in tongues, do you really think God would make them available to *some* of us, but not *all* of us? God forbid!

Every Christian can praise and pray in the tongues that is a *sign* of being filled with the Holy Spirit. And every Christian who does so will experience the help, the blessings, and the benefits that accompany the ability to do so. Amen!

So with that in mind, get filled and let the Holy Spirit make intercession for you!

CHAPTER 7

MIRACLE, MIRACLES, MIRACLES

**And they went out and preached
everywhere, while the Lord kept
working with them and confirming
the message by the accompanying
signs and miracles.
Mark 16:20**

For years I thought the very first miracle that took place after the New Testament church was formed in **Acts 2** took place in **Acts 3** when Peter and John were used by God to heal the lame man who sat at the gate of the temple where they were going for prayer. Whereas that was most certainly a miracle, it wasn't the *first* miracle of the post-ascension era of Jesus and the New Testament church.

The *first* miracle actually took place on the Day of Pentecost when the Holy Spirit *first filled* the twelve apostles* who were gathered in an upper room in Jerusalem (see page 110 for the explanation of why I believe only the twelve apostles were in the upper room on the Day of Pentecost and not 120 people). Some would say that miracle was God filling people with Himself. I certainly would not dispute that. That was indeed a miracle! Every time someone is filled with the Holy Spirit it is a miraculous, supernatural work of God.

But another miracle that took place on that day that operated through people and was witnessed by people was the speaking in tongues. This was a miracle because the tongues they spoke in were languages they had not been taught.

> **And when this sound (tongues)**
> **occurred, the multitude came together,**
> **and were confused, because everyone**
> **heard them speak in his own language.**
> **⁷ Then they were all amazed and marveled,**
> **saying to one another, "Look, are not all**
> **these who speak Galileans? ⁸ And how**
> **is it that we hear, each in our own**
> **language in which we were born?"**
> **Acts 2:6-8**

Those visiting Jerusalem in celebration of the Passover had gathered from many nations and spoke many different languages. In response to hearing the disciples speak in tongues (which was the native language of their home nation), someone from among those visiting asked in amazement how it was that men from Galilee could speak foreign languages without having learned them. The answer is simple: It was a miracle!

The very first miracle performed by the Holy Spirit, manifest through the apostles during the introduction of the New Testament church, was the ability to speak in tongues that were actual, legitimate languages from other places in the world. This is often one of the very first miracles experienced personally by Christians.

The typical effect that miracles have on those who witness them is that it leaves them **"confused"** and **"amazed"** and causes them to **"marvel"** because what they've witnessed defies logic and natural order. It also leaves them without understanding and therefore incapable of explaining what just happened. This is what those who witnessed the miracle of speaking in tongues experienced.

Many today who witness others speaking in tongues without a solid understanding of what's happening are not amazed; instead they are often offended. Some may be confused and may consider those who are speaking in tongues to be crazy **(1 Corinthians 14:23)** because they have had no teaching on the matter. Albeit, there may be some who observe the decent and orderly operation of tongues and are blessed and drawn to God by it.

In fact, this is exactly what took place on the day of Pentecost with those who witnessed Christians speaking in their language. God, being the Master Strategist that His is, deliberately waited until He knew that there would be thousands and thousands of people from all over the world assembled in Jerusalem on the Day of Pentecost while celebrating Passover. God chose that time to perform that miracle because He knew it would get their attention and cause them to be attentive to what Peter would provide as the very first offering of the Gospel of Jesus Christ! And the result of the miracle of them speaking in tongues was three thousand souls believing in Jesus as the Christ and being saved! That's the power of a miracle!

> **This beginning of miracles
> did Jesus in Cana of Galilee,
> and manifested forth His glory;
> and His disciples believed in Him.
> John 2:11 (KJV)**

According to the Bible, turning water into wine during a wedding feast was the first miracle of Jesus as He embarked on His earthly ministry. I find it interesting that John, one of Jesus' disciples, would write that after Jesus performed His first miracle, **"...His disciples believed in Him."** This is interesting because as **"His disciples"** they were already followers of Jesus; and it would be safe to assume that as *followers* they must have already believed in Him. Not only is that safe to assume, I believe that is accurate because typically people don't follow leaders that they don't have some degree of trust and belief in.

There are two viable possibilities. The first possibility is because there were people who saw Jesus perform this miracle, believed in Him because of it, and became disciples. This is a possibility because according to what we find in **John 1**, only Andrew, Peter, Nathanael, Philip, (and possibly John) were believers, followers, and disciples at the time of the wedding feast.

It was not uncommon then (neither is it now) for people to see Jesus perform miracles and begin to follow Him.

> **Then Jesus said to him,**
> **"Unless you people see signs and**
> **wonders, you will by no means believe."**
> **John 4:48**

The other possibility in John writing **"...His disciples believed in Him"** after witnessing the miracle of turning water into wine indicated an even deeper, stronger, more convinced belief than they initially had based on the testimony of others, and other factors. This would be completely understandable because nothing further convinces us and seals our conviction in Jesus being the Christ like witnessing miracles being performed in His name, by the power of God.

MIRACLES ALTER MINDS

It doesn't matter how long a person has been walking with Jesus or how mature they are in Him, seeing a miracle when you've never seen one before will take their belief in Him to higher heights or deeper depths!

This is one of the reasons why having the power of Holy Spirit baptism is so important. Aside from helping people by performing some sort of miracle for them, it serves as a testimony of who the true and living God really is.

I recall having a conversation with a gentleman who was a Muslim. After sharing with him that I was Christian he asked what made me so sure that Jesus was the Messiah. Without having planned to do so (because the conversation itself was unexpected), I began telling him about the miraculous things I have seen and been used by God to be a part of. Before sharing this, nothing else I had said had gotten his attention, probably because he had heard it all before.

But when I began to talk about the miracle-working power of God through the name of Jesus, everything about him changed. His countenance was different; his posture had become one of listening instead of looking for an opportunity to interject. He was engaged and attentive, and he wanted to hear more. He **"marveled"** at the miracle workings of God I shared with him.

His reaction did not surprise me because I don't know of another faith or religion that operates in the miracle-working power of God like Christianity does. And when people see or hear about miracles, as was the case with the people who witnessed Peter and the other apostles speaking in tongues, they know something different, out of the ordinary, and unfamiliar to them is or has taken place and it gets their attention.

I have long said that people may not give much weight to our words about the realness of God and Jesus being the only way to salvation, but when they witness or hear credible testimonies of God's miracle-working power, they take notice! And although they may not receive Jesus in that moment or seemingly receive what you've shared with them about Him, talk of miracles tills the ground of their heart and makes the soil of their soul ready to receive the seed of the Word of God—seed that will bring forth fruit in its season.

IT'S NOT ONLY ABOUT TONGUES

The miraculous ability to speak in tongues that is a *sign* of being filled with the Holy Spirit is important and extremely helpful to us personally. But the power of being filled equips us to perform miracles in the lives of others. And again, when people experience a miracle in their own life or witness such in the life of another, it does more to win them to Christ than ten thousand words! The apostle Paul knew the importance and the persuasiveness of God's power and how its hybrid purpose is to both bless and convince people that Jesus is **"the way, the truth, and the life."** Listen to what Paul wrote in his first letter to the Christians in Corinth:

> **"And I, brethren, when I came to you,**
> **I did not come with excellence of speech or of**
> **wisdom declaring to you the testimony of God.**
> **And my speech and my preaching were not with**
> **persuasive words of human wisdom, but in**
> **<u>the demonstration of the Spirit and of power</u>,**
> **that your faith should not be in the wisdom**
> **of men but in <u>the power of God</u>."**
> **1 Corinthians 2:1, 4-5**

When the apostle Paul founded the church at Corinth, he says he did not do so by using his personal knowledge of the Scriptures, his ability to impress them with his wisdom, or how well he articulated truth. All of those are *natural* things that can be done by most men. But Paul said he came seeking to convince them that Jesus was in fact the Christ, with things no man can do absent of the power of God, and that was *demonstrating* the power of the Holy Spirit through miracles, signs, and wonders!

It's interesting that the very first New Testament church in the book of Acts was established when the power of God was demonstrated by the miracle of tongues *(Peter didn't preach until after that miracle of tongues had been witnessed)*, and the church at Corinth was also established by **demonstration of the Spirit and of power.** I think this has always been the plan of God for His church in winning souls into His kingdom.

But you shall receive power when
the Holy Spirit has come upon you;
and you shall be witnesses to Me
in Jerusalem, and in all Judea and
Samaria, and to the end of the earth.
Acts 1:8

Being "witnesses" for Jesus wasn't just about the apostles' verbal expression of what they were eyewitnesses to. Being "witnesses" for Jesus was also about demonstrating the power of Holy Spirit baptism in miracles, signs, and wonders for people to benefit from, see, believe, and thereby be saved.

When people witness the miracle-
working power of God, it positively
affects their faith in Jesus!

Gideon said to him,
"O my lord, if the Lord
is with us, why then has
all this happened to us?
And where are all His miracles
which our fathers told us about…?"
Judges 6:13

This Old Testament question by Gideon is what I call a *living question*. I call it such because it is a question that is echoed by many Christians in this day and age who are aware of the many stories of miracles told by our forefathers in the faith. Christians who realize that God changes not and that His miracle-working power is the same yesterday, today, and forever! We know that God is the same and His power is unchanged, therefore we wonder in the womb of our mind, **"Where are all His miracles?"**

We have this question simply because we are not seeing New Testament miracles even though we are living in New Testament times. The "greater works" Jesus promised would be done by His disciples (who we are) have seemingly become *lesser* instead of *greater*, especially in America. Yes, we are intellectual and can boast of great theological academic achievements. Yes, many of our fine churches have large memberships and plenty of money. Yes, we have built fine churches with sprawling campuses. But many such places are powerless to pray for those among them and to see them healed from sickness, disease, or other medically incurable conditions.

There are many men and women of God that have never cast out a demon and churches that have never seen a miracle of any sort. Certainly there are churches in America and in other countries where miracles are a common occurrence. But why are there many ministries who have never ministered even one single miracle? There may be a number of reasons for this, but at the top of the list is the reality that the average church in America is not Spirit filled and is therefore not operating with the power of the Holy Spirit.

My prayer has long been for there to be a reawakening of the truth of Holy Spirit baptism so that the body of Christ as a whole can possess the power to change lives and win even more souls!

"Greater works than these shall he do because I go to be with my Father."

The desire of God for His church to be empowered to impact the lives of those who do not yet know Him, as well as those who already have a saving relationship, has not changed. Jesus is *still* baptizing Christians with the Holy Spirit so that we can do the miraculous, and so that the miraculous that we do can sow seeds that will lead to the saving of souls.

Holy Spirit baptism is not an issue of salvation for the person who is Christian. But through boldness, courage, and the anointed miracle-working power of God, Holy Spirit baptism is an issue of salvation for the people God sends across the path of our life. Three thousand souls were saved on the day the first twelve disciples were *filled* and ministered with courage and boldness. And another two thousand were added after the miracle of raising the lame man at the gate of the temple. If you're saved, praise God! But the salvation of someone else could be dependent on your being *filled*.

Are you *filled* with the Holy Spirit? If you are *filled*, you are also empowered to do the miracles Jesus did. Many have placed their faith in Jesus after seeing the miracle-working power of God, but others will see the miracle-working power of God when *we* as Christians place our faith in its ability to perform signs and wonders, and they too will give their life to Christ.

Get filled, have faith, work some miracles, and win some souls!

*Many people believe there were 120 people gathered in the upper room on the Day of Pentecost because Acts 1:15 mentions **"a hundred and twenty"** who were present during the selection of a person to replace Judas. However, there are five things that cause me to believe that on the Day of Pentecost there were only the original eleven disciples and the newly added Matthias who were present when the Holy Spirit first filled believers.

1. In **Acts 1:4, 5** when Jesus commanded them **"not to depart from Jerusalem but to wait for the promise of the Father"** and said that they would be **"baptized with the Holy Spirit not many days from now,"** verse 2 reveals that Jesus was having this conversation with **"the apostles whom He had chosen."**

So the instructions and promise of the soon-coming, first-ever Holy Spirit baptism was made, not to the 120, but to the eleven apostles. And of course, when the twelfth apostle was added, shortly thereafter the Holy Spirit came and filled them.

2. After the final ascension of Jesus to be with the Father, **Acts 1:12** says, **"Then they** (the same eleven apostles Jesus conversed with in verses 4-8) **returned to Jerusalem from the mount called Olivet, which is near Jerusalem, a Sabbath days' journey.** [13] **And when they** (the same eleven apostles) **had entered, they went up into the upper room where they** (the same eleven) **were staying: Peter, James, John, and Andrew; Philip and Thomas; Bartholomew and Matthew; James the son of Alphaeus and Simon the Zealot; and Judas the son of James.** [14] **These** (eleven apostles) **all continued with one accord in prayer and supplication, with the women and Mary the mother of Jesus, and with His brothers."**

This is when we begin to see others mentioned, not in the same place with them, but in prayer with them. Of course we know we don't have to be in the same place together in order to be in prayer together. In fact, **Acts 1:14** and **Acts 2:1** this was the case with the apostles and the others. Acts 1:14 says, **"These all continued with <u>one accord in prayer."</u>** But on the Day of Pentecost, **Acts 2:1** says, **"...they were all with <u>one accord</u> <u>in one place."</u>**

My assertion is that this "**one place**" *was not occupied by all 120 people.* **Acts 1:15** *opens with,* "**And in** those days **Peter stood up…**" *indicating that the day Peter stood up in the midst of the 120 was a different day from when the eleven apostles first entered the upper room upon returning from their final time seeing and being with Jesus.*

It may have also been a different place because it is not very likely that an "*upper room*" *could have held 120 people. This may have been the same upper room that had been prepared for Jesus and the twelve to have their Passover meal on the night He was arrested after having instituted the Lord's Supper.*

Although **Mark 14:15** *states it was a* "**large upper room,**" *large was probably relative to intimately accommodating the thirteen of them. It would make sense for the apostles to return to the place that they shared such an intimate occasion with Jesus before His betrayal and wait for Him to baptize them with* "**the promise of the Father.**"

And even if the 120 were somehow gathered in that upper room, they all probably would not have stayed there together overnight, over the course of the "**not many** days **from now**" *stated by Jesus before the Holy Spirit would come.*

3. Chapter 2 opens with, "**And when the day of Pentecost was fully come…**" *The words* "**the day…was fully come**" *reveal to us that this wasn't the same day in which the 120 were gathered in Acts 1:15. The break between chapters 1 and 2 also indicates a break in time, and on the Day of Pentecost the twelve apostles were gathered in the upper room.*

Support for this is offered in the word "**they**" *of* **Acts 2:1.** "**When** they **were all with one accord in one place…**" *The* "**they**" *that is spoken of is the last group of people mentioned before the word* "**they**" *is offered. In this instance, the* "**they**" *isn't the* "**one hundred and twenty**" *of* **Acts 1:15**; "**they**" *is* "**Matthias…and…the eleven apostles**" *of* **Acts 1:26.**

4. When those who heard them speaking in tongues were wondering what to make of what they were hearing. **Acts 2:14** *says,* "**…Peter, standing up with** the **eleven, raised his voice…**" *It doesn't say that Peter stood up with the 119. The emphasis on the apostles, here and in* *the other noted places, seems to indicate that they were the recipients of the very first filling that took place.*

5. Because God is a God of order, it stands to reason that the leaders of the soon-coming New Testament church would be the first to be baptized in the Holy Spirit before any other believers.

CHAPTER 8

THE TRUSTFUL ABSENCE
OF UNDERSTANDING

For if I pray in a tongue,
my spirit prays, but my
understanding is unfruitful.
¹⁵ What is the conclusion then?
I will pray with the spirit; and I
will also pray with the understanding.
I will sing with the spirit, and I will
also sing with the understanding.
1 Corinthians 14:14-15

A number of years ago I was teaching a series on trusting God and using **Proverbs 3:5** as the platform passage for that teaching. You're probably familiar with the verse that says, **"Trust in the Lord with all your heart, and lean not to your own understanding."** In one of the lessons I recall saying, *"Don't wait until you understand God before you trust Him. True trust is obeying God even when we don't understand what He's doing or where He's leading us."* I learned that this also applies when we are praying in the Spirit without understanding what He's saying when He's praying. We must trust that whatever He's saying when He's praying will cause all things to work out for our good!

CLUELESS

The terms **"pray (and sing) with the spirit"** in verse 15 are very interesting because they further demonstrate how the Holy Spirit, through our born-again spirit man, uses our mouth to offer praise and prayer to God when our mind has no idea of what's being sung or said. *(Yes, when we are Spirit filled we can sing in tongues. And it's beautiful!)*

We know this because of how the term **"with the spirit"** is used in contrast to the alternative possibility, **"with the understanding."** To pray or sing **"with the understanding"** of course means we know or *understand* what we are saying when we are praying or singing because our words are a product of our mind. On the other hand, praying or singing **"with the spirit"** means we *do not* understand the words of the intercession or song because it is the Holy Spirit Who is making those offerings to the Father in a language we have not learned.

Neither the prayers nor the songs are offered through the spiritual *gift* of tongues, but via the tongues that is a *sign* of being filled with the Holy Spirit. When the Holy Spirit is praising or praying to the Father on our behalf it could not be by way of the *gift* of tongues for two reasons: 1) The *gift* of tongues is purposed to "profit" the church, not to praise the Lord; 2) The *gift* of tongues would require the gift of interpretation to accompany it so that the hearers could comprehend what is being said. But God doesn't need an interpreter because He is omniscient; He knows *every* language! In fact, God doesn't need us to speak in any language because He **"understands our *thoughts* afar off,"** and He is a **"discerner of *thoughts* and the intents of the heart."** Long before we set ourselves to say anything to God in any language, He has already interpreted the thoughts of our heart.

So the praying and singing **"with the Spirit"** (as opposed to **"with the understanding"**) is the Holy Spirit praising and praying to God for us through the *sign* of tongues that we're given upon being filled with the Holy Spirit and not the *gift* of tongues.

DISTINGUISHING THE DIFFERENCE

Here is a good way to draw a distinction between the two tongues: When we are praying or praising in the tongues that is a *sign* of being Spirit filled, the Holy Spirit through us is speaking *to God*, **"For he who speaks in a tongue does not speak to men but to God, for no one understands him; however, in the spirit he speaks mysteries" (1 Corinthians 14:2).**
But when the *gift* of tongues is in operation (along with the gift of interpretation), God is speaking *to us*. Isaiah prophesied, **"For with stammering lips and another tongue <u>He will speak to this people</u>" (Isaiah 28:11).**

With tongues the *sign*,
we speak to God.
With tongues the *gift*,
God speaks to us.

During the time that Paul penned these things to the church at Corinth, both types of tongues were a common and important practice in early Christianity. In his letter, Paul wrote to address the issues of tongues (the sign and the gift) and to correct and protect the use of them both. The need for correction seemingly stemmed from some of the Spirit-filled Christians exercising the *sign* tongues that is intended for personal use, in the congregational setting. Paul's concern was not for the large percentage of people who themselves were filled and understood what tongues was about, but for the persons who may have been visiting the church to hear the Gospel of Jesus.

Because these visitors would have been unsaved and unlearned in the matter of tongues, they more than likely would have thought the tongue-speaking Christians to be crazy, refused to return to that or any other church, and maybe even caused to reject Jesus because of what they did not understand. For these possibilities, Paul corrected those who were using the *sign* tongues, that are purposed to bring personal edification, during public service. Even today, we are sometimes accidentally unmindful or inconsiderate of those who may be receiving their first exposure to Christianity or the affect tongues could have on their decision to receive or reject Jesus based upon their experience in our well-meaning church services. We must remember, as much as our services are about us giving God our worship and God giving us His Word, it is more importantly about winning souls to the Savior.

THE IMPORTANCE OF ONES

**"What man of you, having a hundred sheep,
if he loses one of them, does not leave the
ninety-nine in the wilderness, and go after
the one which is lost until he finds it?"
Luke 15:4**

**"Or what woman, having ten silver coins,
if she loses one coin, does not light a lamp,
sweep the house, and search carefully
until she finds it?"
Luke 15:8**

**"Likewise, I say to you, there is joy in
the presence of the angels of God over
one sinner who repents."
Luke 15:10**

Because the Bible reveals the importance of *one* lost sheep, *one* lost coin, *one* lost son, and *one* sinner who repents, shouldn't we view *one* lost visitor as important who may witness the *sign* tongues in operation, not understand, never visit a church again, and never come to salvation? There isn't anything more important than the one person who comes secretly seeking something that they're missing. If Jesus were writing this, I think He'd say that *one* lost soul in need of saving is more important than one thousand people speaking in tongues who are already saved. I think you and I both would agree.

CORPORATE PRAYER IN THE SPIRIT

There is indeed a purpose and a time for corporate prayer in church. When I pastored, once a month we held a night prayer service wherein we would pray for a number of different things. While one person had the microphone praying for their designated prayer agenda item, others were praying in agreement *with the understanding*, while others were praying *with (or in) the Spirit*. The difference between that special prayer service and an ordinary worship service was, those who came understood that service was designated for **"all prayer and supplication,"** including praying in tongues. I don't think we ever had visitors who didn't have an understanding of praying in the Spirit, so unnerving them was never a concern.

Praying in the Spirit is so vitally important that there is a tendency to think that obeying the Word of God by *not* praying in the Spirit during worship service where the unsaved and unlearned will be present will cause us to miss something that God wants to do. However, we will never miss anything the Lord wants to do when we are following the instruction of the Scriptures. Instead, we stand to gain the souls of those who have not been unintentionally discomforted by people all around them speaking in tongues.

> **There will be more joy in heaven over one sinner who repents than over ninety-nine who need no repentance.**

The purpose of this portion of Paul's letter to the Corinthian church was also to protect and defend the proper use of the *gift* of tongues and its co-worker, the gift of interpretation. The apostle understood that the value of these gifts working in tag-team fashion would bring congregational edification to the church without spooking anyone present who was unlearned and unsaved. This is because the interpretation and the explanation of the gifts working in sequential tandem order of, **"by two, or at the most by three, in order, and let one interpret."** This is what Paul meant by, **"Let all things be done decently and in order" (1 Corinthians 14:40).**

In the preceding verse, Paul also provides defense and support for the tongues that is a *sign* of being filled with the Holy Spirit, as well as the decent and orderly use of the *gift* of tongues when he wrote, **"...and do not forbid to speak with tongues."** That is a bold, crystal clear, Holy Spirit inspired statement if there ever was one! *(If Paul had written that in the current era of social media, he may have used all capital letters to emphasize the seriousness of his instruction and the importance of both types of tongues.)* Paul wrote this because he knew there was a possibility of the church leaders overreacting to those who were not speaking in tongues in an orderly manner.

He knew that speaking in tongues without an interpreter could damage the image of the church in the eyes of the unsaved and unlearned; but he also knew that overreacting to that would damage the growth and development of the Christian who makes up the church. So his instruction was for them to not disallow that which was beneficial in building up, but to address that which was undisciplined. As they are to us now, Paul's letter to them was intended to also be a teaching tool. Paul instructed them to not ban speaking in tongues, but teach the people, with his words, how to do so properly.

There are some churches that don't allow tongues to operate simply because they don't think they exist for today or are not for their *type* of church. Well, to the former I say, as long as there is a need for Christians to be built up (and everything else that tongues accomplish), tongues *must* still be available and relevant in helping in these many ways. And to those who say they are not that *type* of church, I would say, if you are a New Testament church that believes in the Father, Son, and the Holy Spirit, you *are* the type of church that will benefit from both tongues the *sign* and tongues the *gift*.

But there are many churches and pastors who do indeed believe in tongues but don't allow them to operate because they are afraid some will be disorderly in their operation of them. First of all, let me say that fear is never a good reason to not do the right thing. Fear is of the enemy and the enemy *always* wants to keep us from doing the right thing.

Secondly, I completely understand the concern about the possibility of people being indecent in the use of tongues. That's when teaching comes in. Most people will respond to sound teaching and instruction. For those who will not, follow the scriptural instructions for dealing with people who are governed by the spirit of disobedience.

> **But if he will not hear you, take with you
> one or two more, that by the mouth of two
> or three witnesses every word may be
> established. And if he refuses to hear
> them, tell it to the church. But if he
> refuses even to hear the church,
> let him be to you like a heathen
> and a tax collector.
> Matthew 18:16-17**

Sometimes unruly people are plants of the enemy that are purposed to cause problems. But some people are simply untaught and without understanding. Teach the undisciplined and deal lovingly with the disobedient, but **"do not forbid to speak in tongues."**

It is of great significance to understand that tongues are no less important today than they were during the first century. In fact, I'm comfortable saying that tongues are even more important consider the condition of the world we're living in and the sin and wickedness we and our loved ones are up against. Paul's admonishment, **"do not forbid to speak in tongues,"** is a part of the *living* Word of God that applies to us as much today as it did in the era of camels and candlelight.

When Paul wrote, **"do not forbid to speak in tongues,"** he wasn't being fanatical or controlling. He was being caring and fatherly because he knew all too well how helpful tongues would be to them individually and collectively as a church. Paul knew the benefits of tongues, not just from spiritual revelation, but also from personal experience. Remember, in this portion of this letter he also said, **"I thank my God I speak with tongues more than you all."** Paul thanked God, not just for the ability to speak in tongues, but for how doing so had benefited him in life and in his spiritual development.

NO GODLY REASON FOR THAT

There is no biblical basis for disputing the fact that tongues are from God. And it goes without saying that anything and everything that is from God is good! This includes every spiritual gift and manifestation of His Spirit. To reject, discourage, or forbid *any* spiritual gift or manifestation of the Holy Spirit, including tongues, is not an idea that is inspired or promoted by God, simply because God would never reject, discourage, or forbid the use of what He gives to benefit and build up His people.

As men and women of ministry, we are in the business of saving souls and helping people to grow. A large part of building people up spiritually is exposing them to biblical truths…truths that we ourselves must sometimes first revisit and embrace.

James 3:1 informs us as men and women of the ministry that **"…we shall receive a stricter judgment."** I believe this not only applies to how we live before God and what we teach His people; I believe it also applies to the helpful truths we're shown that we withhold from His people.

But when we share with the people of God all we know to share, holding nothing back because of personal preference or prejudice, we're being the best possible blessing we can be to the wonderful people the Lord has entrusted to us!

And who doesn't want to be the best blessing possible to a people that God loved enough to send His Son and to give His Spirit?

CHAPTER 9

POWER AND IMPORTANCE

*"And you shall receive power
when the Holy Spirit is come upon you."*
Acts 1:8

The instructions of Jesus in **Acts 1:5** for the disciples to return to Jerusalem and **"wait for the Promise of the Father"** was about them not going forth until they had been armed with that which was needed to aid them, both in ministry and in life.

The "power" would unquestionably serve to help them "be witnesses" of who Jesus is by enabling them to declare the Word of God in ways that were convicting and convincing; and demonstrating the miraculous workings of God in ways that were undeniable and indisputable. These alone would be reason enough to *wait* for the *power* that accompanied being filled, or baptized with the Holy Spirit, but there was more!

The power of the Holy Spirit that is added to our life when we are filled with the Holy Spirit does not only equip us for the ministry of helping others. This power also helps us personally, in many different ways. In fact, this *power* is custom tailored to aid us personally in ways that are fitting for our individual needs. These *needs* could be in the area of our character, our confidence, our courage, our ability to overcome sin and not give in to temptation, our ability to forgive, our ability to trust, our fruit of the Spirit, and the effective operation in our spiritual gifts, talents, and abilities. These are just a few of the ways and things that the power of the Holy Spirit helps us with. I'm sure there are many others.

It was for the sake of the disciples benefiting from the power of the Holy Spirit that Jesus instructed them to **"wait"** and to not go forth in ministry, or life, without first being **"endued with power."** There is a tendency to think that the power was only about their ability to serve effectively in ministry. I think this is because Jesus mentions them being **"witnesses"** for Him in places where they would eventually go and minister the Gospel **"with the Lord working with them** (through the power of the Holy Spirit) **and confirming the Word through the accompanying signs"** **(Mark 16:20).**

But as much as Jesus wanted them to be equipped and empowered for ministry to others, He also wanted them to be equipped and empowered to live *their* lives in victory and in intimate fellowship with God. Jesus knew they would need the power of the Holy Spirit if this were to take place.

Immediately upon being filled, the help of the Holy Spirit's power was demonstrated in the area of ministry and the personal life of the disciples. In fact, the very first thing the Holy Spirit empowered them to do was designed by God to help them personally and in the same moment help them in the ministry of helping others.

The first thing the power of the Holy Spirit empowered the disciples to do was speak in tongues.

> **And they were all filled with the Holy Spirit**
> **and began to speak with other tongues, as the**
> **Spirit gave them utterance.**
> **Acts 2:4**

When the disciples were *first* filled, the *first* power-enabling thing we find them doing is speaking in tongues. This unlearned, miraculous ability to speak in a legitimate language was certainly purposed to serve them personally through all of the ways we've seen how tongues benefits us individually. But that same supernatural ability to speak in tongues was simultaneously being used as a ministry tool, purposed to help others as well.

It goes without saying that God is the most intelligent being to ever exist. His intelligence cannot be rivaled by all of the great minds and computers in the world working together in concert. It also goes without saying that God is the most masterful in the areas of planning and strategies. His superior intelligence, planning, and strategy were on full display on the Day of Pentecost when thousands and thousands of people had gathered in Jerusalem for the annual celebration of Passover.

It was during this gathering of people **"from every nation under heaven"** that the Holy Spirit and the fullness of His power fell as promised on the twelve disciples, enabling them to speak in tongues. Those *tongues*, though foreign to the understanding of the disciples, were able to be understood by those who were visiting Jerusalem, prompting the following questions from someone in the crowd:

> **"...are not all these who speak Galileans?**
> **And how is it that we hear such in our**
> **own language in which we were born?**
> **...we hear them speaking in our own**
> **tongues the wonderful works of God."**
> **Acts 2:7-8, 11**

God, the Master Planner and Supernatural Strategist, did not only use the very first post-ascension miracle to empower and aid the disciples personally. Primarily He used it to minister in getting the attention of those who were not yet followers of Jesus. When they heard the disciples praising God in tongues by declaring His **"wonderful works"** they could not help but to pay attention to Peter as the way had been paved for him to preach the very first post-ascension Gospel message!

It was with the power of the Holy Spirit that this first ministry outreach went forth, resulting in **"three thousand souls"** being added to the Kingdom of our Christ and King, on just their first day of ministry.

But the point is, the first demonstration of the **"power"** Jesus promised (tongues) served to help the disciples personally, as well as those who would benefit from their ministry.

Power to help us,
and power to help us
help others.

Acts 4:1-3
Now as they spoke to the people, the priests, the captain of the temple, and the Sadduccees came upon them, ² being greatly disturbed that they taught the people and preached in Jesus the resurrection from the dead. ³ And they laid hands on them, and put them in custody until the next day, for it was already evening.

Following the miraculous of healing a lame man and another unscripted, unplanned message that brought forth another great harvest of souls, Peter and John were arrested for preaching Jesus and His resurrection. The setting and the scene of their arrest was not an unfamiliar one to them. Both Peter and John were present during the arrest of Jesus, and they both ran, avoided being arrested themselves, and abandoned the Christ.

But things were different. The disciples had something now that they didn't have before. Something that caused them to respond differently during the time of their arrest than they did during the arrest of Jesus. This *something* was the power that was poured upon them when they were baptized with the Holy Spirit just a few days prior.

Aside from the Holy Spirit's power that enabled Peter and John to function effectively in ministry, in this situation we find that same power also personally benefiting them. It hadn't been very long since Peter, in fear for his life, denied Jesus three times after fleeing arrest.

This same Peter, who had previously talked tough from his mind about his come-what-may faithfulness to Jesus but had reflected the fear in his heart when the time came to show his faithfulness, was again in danger of death. This time it was because of his commitment to preach Jesus and Him resurrected, at all costs. But by this time Peter had been empowered to pass the test of courage and commitment he had previously failed.

He was now able to pass the test because the power he received upon being filled with the Holy Spirit personally aided him by adding to him a courage he only *thought* he had previously possessed. And it was in the power of this newfound courage that Peter locked eyes with those who had "**severely threatened them**" to never again "**speak…nor teach in the name of Jesus,**" and said to them:

> "**…whether it is right in the sight of God
> to listen to you more than to God, you
> judge. For we cannot but speak the
> things which we have seen and heard.**"
> **Acts 4:19-20**

I absolutely love that! The *same* Peter who had cowardly avoided being taken into custody was now courageously confirming his commitment to Christ while in custody without any concern for the consequences!

But what was the difference? Again, the difference was the *power* he received after being filled with the Holy Spirit! That power not only allowed him to minister to people, but it also aided

Peter personally in an area where he wasn't very strong prior to being filled. The power of the Holy Spirit aids us in this way also in that it adds to the areas wherein we are lacking, and it helps to strengthen the areas wherein we are weak. Remember, "…**the Spirit also <u>helps in our weaknesses</u>" (Romans 8:26).**

We may be lacking the courage to let people know we are Christians or the confidence to share Christ with others. But the power of the Holy Spirit equips us with the courage and the confidence needed to not be ashamed of the fact that we are Christians, followers of Jesus the Christ! This power also provides us with the boldness to speak up and share Him with others, and defend the Gospel when necessary.

Threats test our trust.
Holy Spirit baptism
empowers us to pass the test!

THE DIFFERENCE MAKER

There is no overstating the fact that Holy Spirit baptism makes a big difference in the life of the individual Christian, the church, the body of Christ as a whole, and the world at large!

Our ability as Christians to have the greatest impact on a world that is wrought with sin, sick, demonically influenced, deceived, and dying, will only come by way of the marriage of love and power. If possible, our only chance to change the course this world is on will be through a union of the love of God and the power of God, working together to give birth to change. The love of God alone won't do it; neither will the power of God alone conceive the change of direction our world is in dire need of. It has to be by way of the matrimony of love and power working together in unity and harmony.

The love of God without the power of God only allows us to have a sympathetic compassion for people who have supernatural needs; needs we cannot meet without the supernatural power of Holy Spirit baptism. However, the *love of God* coupled with the *power of God* enable us to be sympathetic and compassionate while being empowered to bring about change that man, through even his best efforts, is incapable of accomplishing. The power of God flows and operates through the people of God. But it is impossible to be power<u>ful</u> without being Spirit filled. I believe that in rejecting the supernatural manifestation of tongues, we are accidentally and unknowingly repelling the supernatural power of God that meets the supernatural needs of people.

LOVE, COMPASSION, AND POWER

It was the alliance of love, compassion, and power that made the earthly ministry of Jesus so extremely unique and incredibly effective. The love of Jesus caused Him to be compassionate about a person's situation, but it was the power of the Holy Spirit that enabled Him to change their situation. We see this alliance of love and power at work together in the death and subsequent resurrection of the Christ. It was His *love* that caused Him to lay down His life, but it was His *power*, the power of Holy Spirit baptism, that enabled Him to raise Himself up again!

It is this same *love and power* that we as Christians must demonstrate and operate in if we, in these last and evil days, are to tip the scales and win the battles against darkness; a darkness that will only continue to grow darker and darker unless we are fully equipped as the type of light that dispels darkness, instead of the type that is faint, dim, hardly noticeable, and is powerless to drive out darkness.

In **Matthew 5:14** Jesus says of us, **"You are the light of the world."** The purpose of light is not only to be seen or to *see by*; light is also purposed and empowered to damage darkness. As Christians, the power that comes with being *filled* with the Holy

Spirit *empowers* us to do damage to the darkness of sickness, disease, and other ***"works of the devil"*** that Jesus came to destroy but has now called, equipped, and empowered us to destroy!

Being filled with the Holy Spirit and possessing the accompanying power allows us to be the powerful force that light, since the beginning, was created to be. But the absence of individual Christians or Christian churches being filled with the Holy Spirit will result in the believer or that group of Christian believers not being able to operate to the fullest potential.

It is like having a twelve-cylinder car that only operates on six, eight, or ten cylinders. The car is capable of moving and functioning, and it has power and ability to accomplish a great deal of what it exists to accomplish. However, without operating on all twelve cylinders, the vehicle isn't living up to its fullest potential. Sure, it can travel at a speed of 100 mph, but it is designed to travel at a speed of 200 mph, but it cannot because it is not functioning on the optimum ability of all twelve cylinders. It is no different with us as Christians and Christian churches when we're not filled with the Holy Spirit.

Sure, we can do great things, and by all accounts appear to have had a great deal of success. But regardless of how large our churches are, or the number of successful programs and ministries we have, or the number of countries we visit and people we help, if we are not filled with the Holy Spirit according to what we find in the Scriptures, we are not maximizing our potential as Christians or Christian ministries.

If our church has one thousand members and leads five hundred people a year to Christ in other countries, that's great! However, our church could have two thousand members and lead one thousand people a year to Christ in other countries. This is possible because the power of God that accompanies being Spirit-filled Christians and churches adds tremendously to the power of the Gospel that people believe in when they come to Christ, or the power of a pastor's personality, charisma, and academic achievements, or even the power of the congregation's size that draws people into the fellowship.

NOT BAD, JUST, NOT BEST

There isn't necessarily anything wrong with any of these things that commonly draw people to churches. And if any of them have been the reason a church is successful without being Spirit filled, as well as that church is doing, it is operating on less than twelve cylinders and is therefore underachieving. I have long said that one of the greatest enemies of *more success* is *some success,* because *some success* can cause us to think that what we're currently doing has worked to achieve for us the success we have and will therefore lead us to even greater success in the future. But that's not always true. Some things only allow us to succeed to a certain level. But success beyond that level, often, if not always, will require us to be open to learning and implementing new things. New things that will come from increased knowledge or improved knowledge.

It's like a high school athlete who has had a great deal of success on the high school level. If they have aspirations to succeed on the collegiate or professional level, there will be some new and different things they will have to learn and employ in order to enjoy the greater success at the higher level.

Some pastors and churches are satisfied with what they are accomplishing. But there are certain types of pastors who are humble and hungry! Humble enough to acknowledge that they don't know all there is to know about what they know; and they are open to revisiting and receiving something they may have missed before. And their hunger allows not even pride of the *know-it-all* spirit to keep them from feeding on that which can launch them to an ever greater level! A level whereon an even greater height of kingdom success awaits them and their congregation!

This is not necessarily about doing more or giving more. It's about receiving more of what God offers to help us in ministry. Specifically, receiving the scriptural doctrine of Holy Spirit baptism, and in turn receiving the *fullness* of the Holy Spirit. In doing so, the Holy Spirit will add His power and ability to what has already brought us some level of success. Or doing so will bring a level of success to where we have struggled to have any measurable success.

There are many good Christian churches who, despite having prayed for many people to be healed or helped in a miraculous way, have never experienced the supernatural healing or helping power of God that accompanies being filled with the Holy Spirit. They believe in miracles and they know God has the power to perform miracles today like He did in the Bible, but they have not been eyewitnesses or beneficiaries of God's miracle-working power in their life, their ministry, or in their church.

It can be frustrating and faith depleting to pray for people to be healed and no one ever experiences supernatural healing. I'm not talking about healing from a cold, an injury, or something that time, medical attention, or treatment will heal. I'm talking about the healing of things (be they sickness, disease, or a physical or emotional malady) that neither time, medical attention, treatment, nor the finest doctors and their best efforts can heal.

Healing is one of the benefits of having a relationship with the Lord. It is also one of our entitlements through the earthly sacrifice made by Jesus on our behalf.

> **"…who Himself bore our sins in His own**
> **body on the tree, that we, having died**
> **to sins, might live for righteousness—**
> **by Whose stripes you were healed."**
> **1 Peter 2:24**

Jesus very well could have only bled and died for our sins and been resurrected, thereby securing our redemption. But instead, He did more. He allowed His body to be beaten so that our body could be healed. I heard it said, *"Jesus took a beating in His body so that we could have healing in our body."* And it's true. But this is in reference to supernatural healing that is a product of the power of God through Holy Spirit baptism and not by way of natural efforts.

The very first miracle we find being performed through the apostle Peter was the healing of the lame man who was asking alms at the gate of the temple.

> **Peter said, "I do not possess silver**
> **and gold, but what I do have I give to you:**
> **In the name of Jesus Christ of Nazareth,**
> **rise up and walk." [8] With a leap he stood**
> **upright and began to walk; and he entered**
> **the temple with them, walking and**
> **leaping and praising God.**
> **Acts 3:6, 8 (NASB)**

Catch this…Peter said that he didn't have any money to give the man; but then he said, **"but what I <u>do have</u> I give to you…"** What was it that Peter *did have* that was more meaningful than the money the man sought? Peter was in possession of the power of God because he had been *filled* with the Holy Spirit! And it was that power that flowed through Peter as a man of God that healed the man who laid lame near the house of God.

There are pastors and other men and women of God who, despite praying for healing for people in and near the house of God, have never had the supernatural power of God flow through them. But why is it that there have been no miracles in many churches or at the hands of many ministers and pastors? It's a quiet question that lives in the mind of Christians who are aware of what the Bible teaches about miracles of healing, deliverance, and other sorts. It is a question that also sits in silence in the heart of many pastors who have given up on praying for the healing of people because no one was being healed. The primary reason is the absence of the power of God that infuses us during Holy Spirit baptism.

While gathered one last time with His disciples in **Acts 1:4** before He made His final ascension to be with the Father, Jesus "commanded them to not depart from Jerusalem, but to wait for the promise of the Father." This "promise" was the Holy Spirit and the fullness of His power and ability.

IMPORTANT BUT IMPOTENT

The disciples had spent over three years being taught directly from the mouth of the Master, being eyewitnesses to the power of God to heal, cleanse, restore, bind, rebuke, and cast out demons. They had also been commissioned to **"go ye therefore and teach all nations"** and continue doing the things Jesus did. *Still* Jesus instructed them to not go anywhere or do anything until they had first been filled with the Holy Spirit. Why was that? It was because Jesus knew that despite their learning, training, and what they were eyewitnesses to, they needed the power of the Holy Spirit in order to accomplish what He had prophesied and what they had been *partially* prepared for.

And even though they had been authorized to go forth by their commissioning, having the *authority* to do what Jesus did was only part of what they needed to do what Jesus did. Along with the *authority* they needed the *power* of God to make the miraculous take place. Authority licenses us to do certain things, but it's the *power* that equips us to perform those things!

Had they *not* waited and received the power that accompanies Holy Spirit baptism, Peter could have still preached the Gospel on the Day of Pentecost, but it would not have been with the anointing, boldness, or effectiveness that led three thousand souls to the Savior. Neither would the gentleman at the gate of the temple have been healed. Absent of the power of the Spirit, they would have just prayed for him and hoped for the best. But because they trusted, obeyed, stayed, and waited for the promise, they were filled with the power to perform the impossible!

> I have no silver; I have no gold.
> But I have the power of
> the Spirit and it can
> make you whole!

Before Jesus gave the promise of praying to the Father and Him sending the Holy Spirit in **John 14:16**, Jesus first said this in **John 14:12:**

> **"Most assuredly, I say to you,**
> **he who believes in Me, <u>the</u>**
> **<u>works</u> that I do he will do also;**
> **and <u>greater works than these he</u>**
> **<u>will do</u> because I go to My Father."**

The "works" that Jesus is talking about in this verse are not just the good deeds of feeding the hungry, clothing the naked, or visiting the sick and imprisoned. Without question, as Christians we should be doing those types of things because they are demonstrating the heart of Christ and the love of God towards people. But the "works" Jesus is referring to here are also *works* of miracles through the power of Holy Spirit baptism.

Look again at **Matthew 5:16** wherein Jesus goes further in talking about us being **"…the light of the world…"**

> **"Let your light so shine before men,**
> **that they may see your good <u>works</u> and**
> **glorify your Father in heaven."**

Kind deeds and gestures can surely cause people to thank God for the good that has been done through us. But nothing will cause people to **"glorify your Father"** like a miracle!

The Greek word for *glorify* is a word that also means *"to praise, honor, magnify, and celebrate."* When the Lord uses us to perform a miracle for someone through the power of the Holy Spirit, surely they will praise, honor, magnify, and celebrate God. But the Greek word for *glorify* also means *"to think of."* When people experience or witness a miracle in the name of Jesus and by the power of the Holy Spirit, they can't help but *"to think of"* God. And it won't be just a fleeting thought; it's an indelible thought that doesn't easily or ever leave their mind but more than likely draws them to Jesus so that their soul will be saved!

**Authority licenses us
but power equips us!**

**And it came to pass on a certain day,
as (Jesus) was teaching, that there were
Pharisees and doctors of the law sitting by,
which were come out of every town of Galilee,
and Judea, and Jerusalem: and the power
of the Lord was present to heal them.
Luke 5:17**

From my time as a senior pastor until now, wherever I teach the Word of God I pray for healing if I'm given the time and liberty to do so. I pray for healing because of this verse and because one of the purposes behind God giving us power through Holy Spirit baptism is to pray for people to be healed. God wants to heal people. If God did not want to heal *people,* He would have never healed one *person* in the Bible. God healing just one person in the Bible reveals His will to heal. When we are filled we have the healing power of God operating in us and through us.

IMPACT PAKISTAN

On a return ministry trip to Pakistan, before one particular service began, the pastor of that church and I were talking when my host intervened and asked him to tell me of the things that had taken place in a city called Daska, where I ministered one night on my previous trip to Pakistan. For a few reasons, I remember that night very well. The first reason is because we had an extremely difficult time getting to Daska from the city of Sialkot where I was staying.

Although it is only sixteen miles in distance, there had been severe rains and many of the roads were flooded, which made for a very slow and difficult drive. On some roads the water was higher than the wheels on our car, and many cars had stalled and others had been left stranded in the middle of the road. On one of the main streets the water was so high that kids were swimming in it. I'm not talking about the type of swimming I used to do when I was a kid *(maybe an adult, also)* when my feet were on the ground and my arms were going through swimming motions. No, I'm talking about water that was so deep that those kids could not have stood in and kept their head above water.

But I remember that night in Daska also because after teaching the subject of Holy Spirit baptism, someone recorded and sent me a two-minute video clip of people being filled with the Holy Spirit who had responded to the invitation to be filled. It was a blessing for me to view that clip over and over again and to share it with people. But until the moment that I was sitting there with the pastor who helped to organize that meeting, I had not heard anything else about our time together in Daska during my first trip to Pakistan. Then the pastor began to share some things with me at the urging of my interpreter. These are his words:

"By the grace of God, it was a very blessed meeting. Being a pastor I received so many testimonies after that meeting. Many people had cancer and hepatitis. They are healed and their

reports are clear. So there is no hepatitis or cancer anymore in their body. Also, many people received the gift of the Holy Spirit. And two ladies were barren; they didn't have (a) child. One with seven years of marriage, still she was childless; and a second one, after five years of marriage she was still without a child. And after that meeting I received a testimony that they both were pregnant and had a baby. They received that miracle in that meeting. Also, so many testimonies I received about healing pain in ear, headaches, and so many things. The Spirit of the Lord touched so many people. Yes, it was powerful, supernatural. And after three years people still remember that meeting."

I believe there were a number of factors as to why God moved so powerfully in that meeting. But none more important and prevailing than the fact that as I taught on Holy Spirit baptism and people received the teaching and received the baptism of the Holy Spirit, the power that accompanies being baptized in the Holy Spirit was present to heal them! And it did!

But the healing and miracles were products of the power that's provided when we are filled with the Holy Spirit. The Spirit's power has not only impacted Pakistan, but in the many nations I've minister Holy Spirit baptism and prayed for healing, the miracle-working power of the Holy Spirit has positively impacted the lives of thousands of people!

POWER FOR PEOPLE

Many ministers, pastors, and churches have stopped praying for healing. It's not because they don't believe that God can and does heal; it's because they have not seen Him do so in their midst with the members or visitors of their church. The healing power of God operating in our churches is important for a number of reasons. Among them, of course, is the relief of whatever the condition that hinders a person. But another reason is because people come to believe in God and accept Jesus as their Savior when they see the miracle-working power of the Holy Spirit in operation.

In **John 14:10-11** Jesus reveals this truth about the miracle-witnessing power of leading people to faith.

> **"Do you not believe that I am in the Father,**
> **and the Father in me? The <u>words</u> that I**
> **speak to you I do not speak on My own**
> **authority; but the Father who dwells in**
> **Me does the <u>works</u>. ¹¹ Believe Me**
> **that I am in the Father and the Father in**
> **Me, or else believe Me for the sake**
> **of the <u>works</u> themselves."**

Jesus was saying, *"If you don't trust or believe in My <u>words</u>, believe in My <u>works</u>."* Some people are drawn to faith in Jesus simply by the *words* of the Gospel. But for others, they will only be led to faith in God by the miraculous *works* of the Gospel! The *works* of healing, deliverance, people being raised from the dead, blind eyes and closed ears opening, muted mouths beginning to speak, limbs growing, and legs being strengthened to leap when they never before could even walk! These *works* are produced by the power of the Holy Spirit! And it is these types of *works* that pastors and others believe God to perform. Works of miracles that will bless believers and draw unbelievers into a saving relationship with Jesus the Christ!

Jesus says in **John 6:44, "No one can come to Me unless the Father who sent Me draws him…"** What we must realize is that the Father draws people to His Son not only through *words* but also through *works* of miracles. Works of miracles that are produced by the power of Holy Spirit baptism!

THE COLLATERAL IMPACT OF POWER

I can't help but remember the words of the pastor in Pakistan when he said, *"Three years later people are <u>still</u> talking about that meeting!"* It's not just the fact that people are still talking about that meeting; it's, <u>who</u> they are talking about that meeting *to*. In a country that is over 95 percent Muslim, *that's* who people are talking to about that meeting and the power of the Holy Spirit that healed and filled people and Jesus the Christ who made it all possible! There isn't any doubt in my mind that many people gave their heart to Jesus that night, and many more did so after witnessing, hearing about, and seeing the miraculous manifestation of what was testified to!

And a great multitude followed Him,
<u>because they saw His miracles</u> which
He did on them that were diseased.
John 6:2 (KJV)

When we as members of the five-fold ministry offices are filled with the Holy Spirit and have the power of God to heal and do other miraculous things in the name of Jesus, not only are we being a blessing to the recipients of the miracles, but we are also helping to spread the Gospel through the words of their testimony to others about what the Lord has done for them. The importance of testimonies cannot be understated or underestimated because people overcome the devil *"...by the blood of the Lamb, and by the word of their testimony..."*

OMNIPRESENT POWER

The power of God that is promised to us at the filling of the Holy Spirit doesn't only work to do the miraculous in church for members or visitors. *(In fact, oftentimes God heals or performs some other type of miracle for unbelievers. He does so, so that they will believe in Jesus, and so that they will go and testify to others so that they will believe in Jesus too!)* God will use the power of the Holy Spirit through us wherever we go. For a number of years I ministered every Tuesday at the Riverside County Jail in Riverside, California. As was my custom, after teaching the Word of God I extended an invitation for people to receive Jesus, be filled with the Holy Spirit, and to receive prayer for healing.

One day I received a letter from one of the inmates who sat in one of the meetings that read:

"I hope this letter reaches you in the very best of health and spirits. You probably don't remember me. I was going to your services in (the) Riverside County Jail. I was in 5A. I'm the guy you prayed for over my liver. Well, I got tested over here and the doctor told me my liver is in perfect health. I can't believe it got better. Just two years ago they said I had cirrhosis. I believe prayer worked. Thank the Lord! And thank you too!"

The power we are endued with when we are filled with the Holy Spirit works wherever we are because it accompanies us wherever we go. Whether we are in church, in the county jail (visiting or staying a while), or in the hospital praying for someone. Take a look at this testimony from a woman who is a wife and mother of four and was a member of the church I pastored.

"I just wanted to share my testimony on the wonderful healing power of God. When I was in the hospital with a brain tumor, you came to lay hands and pray for me. Two days later I was released from the hospital because the doctors said the surgery they had planned for me was no longer necessary because somehow my tumor had just vanished. They called it some kind of phenomena, but I told them it was the power of prayer and the faith in that prayer that the Lord has healed me. One of the doctors said that he had been in the medical profession for twenty-one years and that he had seen a lot of unexplainable

things and that he would not rule out prayer. I have been tumor-free for ten years now and I thank God for each day that He has given me. May this testimony be a blessing to those going through any kind of health issues."

This woman was miraculously healed from this brain tumor not because she was a Christian and a church member. Neither was she healed because as a pastor and *her* pastor I went and prayed for her. Her healing was a product of the grace of God and the miracle-working power of His Holy Spirit!

> **"The surgery they had planned was no longer necessary...my tumor had just vanished!"**

The power of the Holy Spirit isn't a power that has been ordered to occupy a place; it is a power that has been poured out upon and occupies people who have received the baptism of the Holy Spirit. And it is through the name of Jesus that this power is released to perform what no one or nothing else is capable of performing.

Jesus told the disciples to wait for the promise because He knew they would need the power of that promise to do the work of the ministry in the way He did—with compassion, courage, confidence, boldness, and life-impacting power! The words of Jesus to His disciples back then are living words for you and me as modern-day disciples.

You need this power in your life so you can impact the lives of people the Lord will place on your path. Yes, the Lord has called us to salvation, but He has also called us to service—the service of helping others! Some of the most lasting and impactful ways we will help people will require us to be filled with the power of Holy Spirit baptism!

If you have yet to be filled with the Holy Spirit but desire to be filled, keep reading! The final chapter of this book will lead you through the process of becoming filled, empowering you to impact people for the Kingdom of our Christ and King!

CHAPTER 10

BECOMING FILLED

**And they were all
filled with the Holy Spirit
and began to speak with
other tongues, as the
Spirit gave them utterance.
Acts 2:4**

I share God's desire for you to experience and live in the fullness of everything that Jesus lived, died, and rose again for. And that which He has promised us—including the baptism of the Holy Spirit. This work of love and grace not only empowers, prepares, and equips us to be the boldest, strongest, most committed, and impactful Christians we can possibly be, but it also fills us with as much of God as anyone can possibly have.

If you were not filled with the Holy Spirit (according to the pattern provided in the Holy Scriptures) or have not been baptized with the Spirit during the course of reading this book, I hope you are willing and ready to receive this empowering work of God today.

This chapter is purposed to guide you through the steps that will lead you to being filled with the precious Holy Spirit of God. There are five simple keys I share in leading people to being Spirit filled. I will share them briefly and go a little deeper into each of them as the chapter progresses.

1) Be saved
2) Believe
3) Desire
4) Ask
5) Speak

<u>**BE SAVED**</u>

This simply means that you have repented from sin and confessed your faith in Jesus as your Savior. Remember, it is possible to be saved but not yet filled, but it is impossible to be filled if we're not yet saved.

I recall the time when I was ministering Holy Spirit baptism to an individual, walking them through this process, but they were not being filled. I tried two or three times before the Spirit said to me, *"Lead them in the prayer of salvation."* I did so and walked them through the process again and they were filled instantly!

I already knew that being saved was the number-one requirement in being filled *(because the Holy Spirit is not going to fill or even dwell in a temple that doesn't belong to the Lord),* but what I learned was that not everyone who seeks to get filled is already saved, though they may think they are. To remedy this, when I minister to groups large or small, in America or abroad, I always lead the entire group in the prayer of salvation. Though many may already be saved, it doesn't hurt for them to repeat that prayer, but it's a tremendous help for those who are not yet saved.

If you have not yet repented from your sin and accepted Jesus as your Savior, in sincerity, simply say:

**Father, I believe that Your Son
Jesus came to earth, died on
the cross for my sins, and rose again.
I receive Jesus as my Savior, now.
Father, please forgive me of my sins.**

I repent and vow to serve You
all the days of my life.
Thank you, Father.
In Jesus' name. Amen.

(If you have said this prayer for the very first time, congratulations!
Jesus has become your Savior! Now allow Him to also be the Lord of
your life by living in obedience to His Word! It'll be worth it!)

If you are under the impression that you are already saved and
didn't pray this prayer but have trouble receiving the baptism of
the Holy Spirit after following the steps that follow, there's nothing
wrong with coming back and going before the Father with this
prayer. Afterwards, follow the process of being filled again.

BELIEVE

Another key to becoming filled with the Holy Spirit is believing.
Everything God does is through grace and faith— be it our faith or
those who are interceding for us. Twenty-two times in **Hebrews 11**
we find God having moved **"through faith"** or **"by faith,"** indicating that **He brings promises to pass, performs miracles, or**
rewards His children in some way or with something according
to what we are believing Him for.

In **Acts 1:4, 5**, Jesus says Holy Spirit baptism is a **"promise of**
the Father." This promise, like the promises received by Enoch,
Noah, Abraham, and others, is also received by us, **by faith.** By our
belief that there is more of God's Spirit to be had, He will respond
to our faith and fill us with His Spirit.

Christ has redeemed us from the curse
of the law, having become a curse for us
(for it is written, "Cursed is everyone who
hands on a tree"), [14] that the blessing

> **of Abraham might come upon the**
> **Gentiles in Christ Jesus, <u>that we</u>**
> **<u>might receive the promise of</u>**
> **<u>the Spirit through faith</u>.**
> **Galatians 3:13-14**

Let's consider two things from these two verses. The first is, the apostle Paul saying, **"...might receive the promise of the Spirit..."** to the **"churches of Galatia" (verse 2)** reveals that he knew it was very possible that some of the Christians in those *churches* had not yet received **"the promise of the Spirit."** Paul was not saying they had not received the *indwelling* of the Spirit that takes place immediately with every Christian. He was talking about the promise of Holy Spirit baptism.

Let's look again at **Acts 1:4-5:**

> **And being assembled together with them,**
> **(Jesus) commanded them not to depart**
> **from Jerusalem, but to wait for the <u>promise</u>**
> **<u>of the Father</u>, "which," He said, "you have**
> **heard from Me; [5] for John truly baptized**
> **with water, but you shall be <u>baptized with</u>**
> **<u>the Holy Spirit</u> not many days from now."**

When the apostle Paul writes about **"the promise of the Spirit"** he is talking about it in terms of being baptized in the Holy Spirit, and not merely having a measure of the Spirit, which again, is given to every believer at the moment of their new birth in Christ.

The second point to consider in this passage is that Paul says the way to **"receive the promise of the Spirit (is) through faith."** By believing what the Bible reveals about Holy Spirit baptism, desiring to receive Holy Spirit baptism, *seeking* the filling of Holy Spirit baptism, and expecting to receive the baptism of the Holy Spirit. A *measure* or the basic *indwelling* of the Spirit is an innate part of our faith in Jesus as Savior; but the *filling* of the Spirit comes by faith.

Hebrews 11:1 says, "...<u>faith is</u> the substance of things <u>hoped for</u>..." *Hope* is *confident expectation*. Nothing reveals the presence of *faith* like *confidently expecting* to receive what God has promised. Even when the promise seems to be suspended in its arrival, *faith* continues to seek with the *confident expectation* of finding.

DESIRE

Another essential element in receiving the fullness of the Holy Spirit is having a genuine desire for it. *Desire* is an inward longing that prompts the outward action of *asking*. **"Whatever things you <u>desire</u> when you <u>pray</u> (ask God) ..."** Notice the order, *desire* followed by *asking*. When we have a *desire* for something but do not possess the means or have the ability to make it happen, we *ask* someone to help us to receive or achieve that which we desire.

If you *desire* to be baptized in the Spirit, the next step is to simply *ask* the Father to fill you with the Holy Spirit. Remember, **"...your heavenly Father will give the Holy Spirit to those who <u>ask</u> Him."**

Hebrews 11: 6 says that God is a **"rewarder of those who diligently seek Him."** Because God *is* the Holy Spirit, when we *seek* to be filled with the Holy Spirit it is because we *desire* to know and experience God in an even greater way.

When our desire causes us to ask and seek, our asking and seeking will cause us to find and possess. Listen to what our God says in **Jeremiah 29:13:**

> **And you will *seek* Me <u>and find Me</u>,**
> **when you search for Me with all your heart.**

Not only do we seek because we desire to find, but *when* we seek God He guarantees that we will *find* Him because He hides Himself in plain view. In like manner, when we desire and seek

God for His Spirit to fill us, His Spirit will be found by us, and It will in fact *fill* us!

> When our desire causes
> us to seek God,
> our seeking will cause
> us to find God.

ASK

Luke 11:9-13
So I say to you, ask, and it will be given
to you; seek, and you will find; knock,
and it will be opened to you. [10] For everyone
who asks receives, and he who seeks finds,
and to him who knocks it will be opened.
[11] If a son asks for bread from any father
among you, will he give him a stone?
Or if he asks for a fish, will he give him a
serpent instead of a fish? [12] Or if he asks
for an egg, will he offer him a scorpion?
[13] If you then, being evil, know how to
give good gifts to your children, how much
more will your heavenly Father give
the Holy Spirit to those who ask Him?

Ask, seek, and knock all indicate *desire*. Typically, we ask for what we desire to have, we seek what we desire to find, and when we knock we desire that the door be opened for us.

Many (including myself in times past) have taught this passage having only to do with prayer. And while asking, seeking, and knocking are most certainly elements of prayer, this particular portion of the prayer lesson taught by Jesus to the disciples is specifically about receiving the Holy Spirit.

We know this because verse 13 concludes with Jesus saying the Father gives **"the Holy Spirit to those who ask Him."** So, even though verses 11-13 is offered on the heels of providing a format for prayer and talking about the importance of persistence in prayer, Jesus concludes indicating that, with all there is to ask, seek, knock, and pray about, the one thing we must not be amiss about asking and seeking the Father for is the Holy Spirit.

In fact, what I find to be very interesting is, the Holy Spirit is the *only* thing Jesus specifically encourages us to ask the Father for. In other places when He tells us to ask the Father for things, it is always general. For example:

> **"…if two of you agree on earth concerning
> <u>anything</u> that they *ask*, it will be done
> for them by My Father heaven."**
> **Matthew 18:19**

> **"Therefore I say to you, <u>whatever</u> things
> you ask when you pray, believe that you
> receive them, and you will have them."**
> **Mark 11:24**

In these two verses, Jesus teaches about prayer and He presents a blank prayer request form. But in Luke's account of the *ask, seek, and knock* teaching on prayer, Jesus fills one of those prayer request forms for us, urging us to ask the Father for the Holy Spirit.

Again I ask…why would Jesus urge us to ask for something that occurs independent of our participation? The fact that He tips us off to asking the Father means that there is more of the Holy Spirit to be had that doesn't accompany receiving Christ. More that the Father will freely give us simply for the asking!

> The Father will give
> the Holy Spirit to
> them who ask Him.

SPEAK

Remember, the evidence of being filled with the Holy Spirit is *speaking* in tongues! You should not expect a warm or fuzzy feeling. If you have a warm and fuzzy feeling before you start the process, you should probably sober up and repent before you go forward.

(*I'm sorry! I couldn't resist! But the Bible does say,* **"Don't be drunk with wine but be filled with the Spirit."**) You should not expect to *feel* anything; neither should you expect to hear angels singing or to fall out!

When I've ministered Holy Spirit baptism to people, if they fell to the floor when I laid hands on them, I requested them to be picked up and continued the process because falling out isn't a sign of being filled with the Holy Spirit.

When people were baptized in the Spirit in the Scriptures, we don't find anyone falling out or feeling fuzzy. Instead, what we find consistently is that **"they spoke in other tongues as the Spirit gave them utterance."**

The words, **"they spoke,"** are key. In order for *us* to begin to speak in the unlearned language the Spirit enables, *we must speak!* There are times when I've walked people through the process and we arrive at the point when I ask them to lift their hands and begin to speak but their lips remain sealed! I continue to encourage them to speak because what is being poured in at the filling cannot come out unless we speak! (*I prefer for them to speak anything aside from their natural language, but sometimes words of praise like "Hallelujah!" or "Thank You, Jesus!" can also lead to praising in the Spirit.*) This will be required of you as well. After you ask the Father to fill you and you lift up your hands and expect to speak in tongues, *you* have to begin to speak.

Speak up and speak out, please!

PROVEN PROCESS

Sometimes, as we have seen with the new Christians of Cornelius' house in **Acts 10**, God will pour His Spirit on people absent of any outward effort on their behalf. But more often than not, it has been my experience in ministering Holy Spirit baptism for over twenty years to people in countries throughout the world that Jesus baptizes Christians with the Holy Spirit in response to our faith, our desire to be filled, our asking to be filled, and our speaking.

WE ARE NOT IGNORANT OF HIS DEVICES

What I am about to share with you is nothing to be afraid of. It is simply something to be aware of in your quest to receive the baptism of the Holy Spirit.

Holy Spirit baptism is such a threat to the devil, his kingdom of darkness, and his agenda to **"steal, kill, and destroy,"** that he may put up some resistance or place some obstacle on your path towards being filled.

Once you accept what the Bible teaches about being baptized _with_ the Holy Spirit (its difference from being baptized _by_ the Holy Spirit, the possibility of being saved and not yet filled, tongues as a *sign* of being filled, etc.), have a desire to be filled, and seek to be filled, the devil may try to distract you from being filled, delay you from being filled, or he may try to cause you to doubt being able to be filled.

Of the devil's tactics of distraction, delay, and doubt, I would say that his strategy of choice is *doubt*. The devil's go-to game plan is doubt because he has had a great deal of success in depriving people of promises, answered prayer, and other kingdom entitlements. In fact, *doubt* was the scheme the devil first used when he showed up on the scene in the Garden of Eden. The devil used doubt to trick Adam and Eve into eating from the tree in the middle of the garden, thereby depriving them of a great deal of what God desired, promised, and had planned for them.

Because *doubt* has served Satan well, it is his tactic of choice in keeping people apart from the good things God has in store for them—including the baptism of the Holy Spirit.

In just a moment I am going to encourage you to go into prayer and **"ask"** the Father to give you the Holy Spirit. And I will share with you the process I've used countless times all over the world in leading people to being filled.

I have learned that it is during the process, or the prayer, or while waiting for God to fill people, that the devil strikes with the *fiery darts* of doubt. These doubts are thoughts that say things like, *"This isn't for you."* Or, *"You are already filled; you don't have to speak in tongues to prove it to anyone."* Or, *"You sound silly trying to speak in tongues."* Or, *"People are looking and you are making a fool of your-self."* Or, *"You have too much sin in your life. You are not worthy. God is not going to give His Holy Spirit to an unholy person like you."* Or, *"This is not working. Try again later."* Or some other lie.

What I tell people to do that is very effective in warding off the fiery darts of doubt and condemnation of the devil is to simply say in their mind, *"In the name of Jesus, the Father is filling me with His Holy Spirit."*

I tell people to say this in their mind because the mind is the place of warfare where the devil launches his attack with his darts of doubt. So it is on this same battleground of our mind that we must thwart the darts of doubt with words of affirmation, declaring the desire of God and the promise of God that is found in the Word of God!

Remember, when Jesus encountered the devil in the wilderness and the devil launched an attack on the mind of Jesus with ungodly words, ideas, and suggestions, Jesus answered back with the Word of God each time saying, **"It is written…"** in response to whatever the devil was saying. If the devil launches an attack with thoughts of doubt in your mind, in your mind attack back with the Word of God. Say, *"It is written that the Father will give me the Holy Spirit because I've asked Him."* Or, *"It is written that I shall receive the promise of the Father through faith."* Or, *"It is written, Jesus baptizes me with the Holy Spirit. I shall be filled!"*

Fight back in your mind by reaffirming what you have learned from the Word of God concerning God's desire and promise to baptize you with His Holy Spirit! Your use of God's Word will cause you to triumph over the fiery darts of the devil, and you shall be filled!

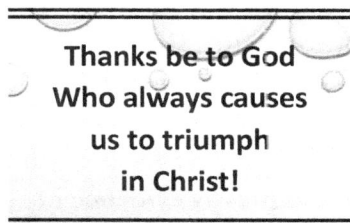

**Thanks be to God
Who always causes
us to triumph
in Christ!**

The filling of the Holy Spirit can take place as soon as you lift your hands and begin to speak. But for the sake of not doubting, becoming discouraged, or siding against the role tongues play in being filled, it is important to understand that sometimes it may take a few minutes. On occasion, it may take a little longer. This was the case with me as I wasn't filled and began to speak in tongues until the following morning when I was in prayer. I have even heard accounts of it taking a couple of weeks. I don't know why that was the case, but the important thing is to not allow your faith to be depleted if it doesn't happen right away or in the next few days. Don't distrust or be dismayed. Just keep believing; it'll happen!

PRAYER

Here is the prayer I have used for many years and in many countries in leading people to being filled with the Holy Spirit. It will work for you as it has worked for thousands of other people. After repeating this prayer *(it doesn't have to be word for word, just the gist of it)*, lift your hands and begin to speak.

HOLY SPIRIT BAPTISM PRAYER

Father, Your Son Jesus said that You would give the Holy Spirit to them that ask You.

So I am asking You now, in the name of Jesus, to please fill me with Your Holy Spirit.

I fully expect to speak in tongues as evidence of me being filled.

**Please fill me now.
In Jesus' name.
Thank You, Father. Amen.**

LAST BUT NOT LEAST

There is one final point of extreme significance I want to share with you. And that is, when you get filled and begin to speak in tongues, don't let that be the only time you speak in tongues. Remember, tongues are a tool that helps to build us up. And it is also one of the weapons of our warfare that we can use against the forces of darkness. But no tool or weapon can effectively do what it is purposed to do if we only use it one time or sparingly. How far do you think a carpenter building a house will get if he only uses his hammer one time? Or how long will it take him if he only uses his hammer once a month? How victorious do you think a military man or woman will be if they only use their weapon once in a war when their enemies are using everything in their arsenal against them?

Once you *receive* the Holy Spirit and are able to praise and pray in tongues, do it on a regular basis! Preferably daily! It doesn't have to be for very long periods of time. It may be for only a minute or two. But a minute or two of the Holy Spirit interceding for us can accomplish more than a minute or two of us praying for ourselves or others. Remember, you can start and stop whenever you choose. Which means that you can begin speaking in tongues while you're walking, bike riding, or driving your car.

And if you want to multitask…that's right, you can pray in the Spirit while you read your Bible, your favorite book, or the newspaper. *(It's definitely a good idea to pray in the Spirit while reading the newspaper!)* But the key is to take advantage of the Holy Spirit's desire to help us with our weaknesses, pray for things and people we don't know to or how to pray for, and to build us up on our most holy faith!

The more we praise and pray in the tongues that is a *sign* of being filled, the more we allow the Holy Spirit to help us while doing so!

In Conclusion

I trust that this book has been a blessing to you and that you will not only benefit from it personally, but will also share what you have learned with others. God doesn't teach us *only* for the sake of us learning. He teaches us so that we in turn will teach others what we have learned. This is how we as disciples, make disciples!

If you have not done so already, go before the Father in prayer and simply *ask* Him to give you His Holy Spirit. When you ask, you *shall* receive! And after you have been blessed to receive the Holy Spirit, go and be a blessing to others with all of the power, authority, and anointing that accompanies, being *Filled*!

ABOUT THE AUTHOR

With pronounced spiritual gifts of teaching, discernment, and exhortation, and with an entertaining sense of humor and use of everyday examples, K. Sheldon Bailey's ministry of the Word of God is insightful, revelatory, challenging, enjoyable, and extremely helpful to the Christian who endeavors to establish or strengthen their personal relationship with God through Jesus Christ.

K. Sheldon Bailey's thirty years of committed Christian living, which includes eleven years of past senior pastor experience, compassionately causes him to minister with the heart of a shepherd and relate to believers on every level of their Christianity.

With over twenty-five years of experience in ministering to men in Sunday school, Bible studies, the county jail, and in one-on-one settings, K. Sheldon possesses an innate ability to communicate with men and a passion for their overall well-being that enables him to effectively encourage, inspire, and edify Christian men of all ages and backgrounds.

A worshiper who honors and takes great pleasure in the presence of God, K. Sheldon values the music ministry and every ministry of the arts. He is an amateur percussionist, an inspired lyricist, and a novice playwright.

As a single Christian, K. Sheldon Bailey supports, practices, and teaches sexual abstinence and the blessings and benefits that accompany such a lifestyle.

In his quest of *"Taking the Word, Teaching the World,"* ministry trips have taken K. Sheldon on more than one occasion to the countries of Pakistan, Zimbabwe, Zambia, Uganda, Rwanda, Kenya, Germany, Poland, the Czech Republic, India, Haiti, and South Africa. A Chicago native, K. Sheldon Bailey currently resides in Southern California.

K. Sheldon Bailey is also the author of ***Trouble: What Every Christian Should Know About Trials, Tribulations, and Troublesome Times.*** *Trouble* is a book for the ages! Laced with lessons learned from the lives of Bible characters such as Joseph, Job, David, Daniel, Peter, Paul, Jesus the Christ, and others, *Trouble* is a tremendous tool that will greatly aid you in overcoming seasons of trials and tribulations of any sort!

TAKE A LOOK BELOW AT WHAT PEOPLE HAVE SAID ABOUT *TROUBLE*!

"K. Sheldon Bailey is a good Bible teacher. In Trouble, *he writes with pragmatic insights on understanding trouble, how it is used by God to shape and equip us inwardly, and how to remain rooted in Christ until trouble's purpose is complete.*

This book is certain to encourage you while providing proven biblical instructions on how to triumph over trials and tribulations and live in the fruitfulness of victory and destiny!"

Sam Chand, Leadership Consultant and Author of
Bigger Faster Leadership

"K. Sheldon Bailey addresses the topic of Trouble *head-on! He also gives hope to anyone seeking answers for dealing with the difficult times of life.* Trouble *takes a biblical and practical approach to using God's Word and our faith in not getting weary but learning how to overcome. This book will be an insightful study for anyone."*

Ed Smith, Bishop of Zoe Association of Churches, Whittier, CA, and CEO of Awayken.com

"K. Sheldon Bailey's book Trouble *turns the topic of trials and tribulations upside down and inside out! Biblically based and filled with scriptural revelation...the insights, practical advice, and godly encouragement will lift your mind and spirit and equip you to triumph over trouble!*

Rev. Dr. Georgia A. Hill, Esq.

"What a great book on a subject that no one is immune to! Trouble *takes a biblical approach to dealing with trials and tribulations in ways I had never considered. Moreover, K. Sheldon Bailey insightfully expresses things in a clear and concise way that made me say, 'Yes, that's right!'*

The truths of Trouble *help us understand the trying times that come our way and how to handle them God's way! Please take time to read this book. No matter where you are in your spiritual walk with Christ,* Trouble *will bless you!"*

Lew Wilson, VMI, Inc.

"K. Sheldon Bailey's book, Trouble, *has been a tremendous resource for me. Initially, I bought it to support him, but little did I know what a great support* Trouble *would be to me as I faced various difficulties in my life.*

Trouble *is filled with godly wisdom and God's Word is shared in meaningful ways that spoke to me about my trials. Every few pages I found something that spoke to me about my current circumstances or the circumstances of a close friend or family members.*

Trouble *also helped me to share godly wisdom with others who were and are in need. And it gave me great encouragement to soldier on in the service of our King!*

I wholeheartedly encourage you to get Trouble, *and savor the journey through it!"*

Dixon Hinderaker, Innovative Technologies

To order *Trouble* go to:

KSheldonBailey.org
Amazon.com
BarnesandNoble.com

Made in the USA
Las Vegas, NV
17 July 2025

25059816R00105